The APOCALYPTIC HEART

The Book of Revelation in an unjust world

Ron Browning

WIPF & STOCK · Eugene, Oregon

Wipf and Stock Publishers
199 W 8th Ave, Suite 3
Eugene, OR 97401

The Apocalyptic Heart
The Book of Revelation in an Unjust World
By Browning, Ron
Copyright©2015 by Browning, Ron
ISBN 13: 978-1-4982-3097-1
Publication date 5/13/2015
Previously published by Morning Star Publishing, 2015

All rights reserved. Other than for the purposes and subject to the conditions prescribed under the *Copyright Act*, no part of this publication may be reproduced, stored in a retrieval system, or transmitted in any form or by any means, electronic, mechanical, photocopying, recording or otherwise, without the prior permission of the publisher.

Book design: John Healy
Cover image: *Landmine victim mother and child* painted by Maung Maung Tinn based on a photo by Yuzo Uda

Yuzo Uda was born in Kobe, Japan, in 1963. After studying photography in Boston, he began his career as a photojournalist, covering the civil war in El Salvador from 1990-92 as a freelancer. Focusing on Southeast Asia and Central America, he continued to document life under military rule, the lives of indigenous peoples, and global poverty. In 1995, he studied at the Graduate School of International Cooperation Studies at Kobe University, receiving a master's degree in international law.

for
David Townsend S.J.
scriptural exponent and friend

The Apocalypse is our life.
　　　　　　　　　　Fr Tom Hopko, Orthodox Church in America

I look out on the ocean, the immensity of God and the vastness of his Coming.
　　　　　　　　　　St Simeon the New Theologian, 6th cent.

This is the end of the beginning of my life.
　　　　　　　　　　Dietrich Bonhoeffer, before being hanged, 1945

You wept over Jerusalem, O Christ, see now your prophecy extend, as we enter the eclipse of our God.
　　　　　　　　　　Jim Cotter

If you get there before I do ... tell my brothers and sisters I am coming there too.
　　　　　　　　　　Negro Spiritual

Contents

Introduction 9

Based on the Text   11

Chapter One 13
    Receiving the Vision

Chapter Two 23
    Picturing John on Patmos

Chapter Three 31
    Re-Awakening to Christ in the Midst

Chapter Four 39
    Facing Systemic Evil

Chapter Five 51
    Anticipating the Kingdom

Chapter Six 61
    Accompanying the Martyrs

Chapter Seven 69
    Silencing the Soul

Chapter Eight 77
    Witnessing the Structures Fall

Chapter Nine 85
    Responding to the Books Opened

Chapter Ten 91
    Delighting in the Consummation

BROADER CONSIDERATIONS   99

Chapter Eleven 101
    Love and Justice

Chapter Twelve 107
    The Apocalyptic Heart

Chapter Thirteen 109
    Inquiry: Nick's Questions

Chapter Fourteen 113
    Life-Themes

Glossary 119
Selected Bibliography 121

Introduction

Blessed are those who hear this prophecy and take it to heart. 1:3

In these meditations the interpretation of the book of Revelation that I will use is based on the directions of some current scholarship, especially as it comes to us from contexts of oppression. Eastern Orthodox understandings will also help in this endeavor. The vision that John the writer records is both profoundly political and spiritual.

In most discussions about how to interpret Revelation, it is the cataclysms that become the main issue in question. My conviction is that the interpreters that I make use of here are able to see clearly what the cataclysms in the text actually mean.

It is helpful, therefore, to know from the start what good interpretation of the book is and what it is not. I offer these simple guidelines as a framework in the hope that they will help you, the reader, both with the chapters that follow and with your own reflective reading of the text of Revelation:

1. **The Risen Christ** stands at the centre of the vision. The centre of the vision is not the catastrophes. He is the sacrificed Lamb and he stands as a unique figure in human history as the redeemer, having dramatically shifted its course towards deconstruction and reconstruction.
2. The **symbolic nature** of the vision described needs to be emphasised whilst reflecting on the text. We do not read the events that John sees as literally happening (Rev.4ff). They represent something.
3. **The catastrophes** represent the destructive forces that have been happening in the course of history - past and present. They are not telling us what is about to happen in the future (of our history). Yet, they will continue into the future and intensify (see #6).
4. **The numbers** are to be understood symbolically, not literally.

5. John's vision is **prophecy**, as he informs us. It is not a set of predictions of future history in any detail. As prophecy, he is presenting a picture to the churches of his time and in each generation that is to challenge and encourage believers in their faith and action. That is what biblical prophecy always does.
6. There is a second meaning to the catastrophes. They represent **the clash** between the decision of God - based on the victory of the Lamb - and the forces of evil, finally to defeat them and culminate history. They are not displaying a God punishing humanity. God loves the Creation, as the cross of Christ displays, and will bring it to its completion, with mercy and justice.
7. John's encouragement to believers is to **be strong** because they will overcome the evils at hand, which may result in the eventuality of dying for their faith. They participate in the drama of history coming to its close. They are not bystanders. The witness and the prayers (in life and in death) of the saints and martyrs will hasten the coming of the Consummation.

The whole text is a letter written by John to the churches. The initial hearers of the letter did not need a framework like the one I am suggesting here. Their historical setting provided the framework. They understood the letter accordingly. But today, in a different setting, we need a framework.

Each chapter of the first section of this book is introduced by a verse from Revelation in order to act as a window into a key topic of John's vision; I then proceed to discuss the meaning of that topic for our lives today. In the second section broader apocalyptic themes are explored.

My own experience of working with refugees in recent years is brought into the reflections to provide examples and help anchor the topics within today's world.

BASED ON THE TEXT

Chapter One

Receiving the Vision

When I saw him, I fell at his feet as though dead. He then placed his right hand on me and said, "Do not be afraid, I am the first and the last." 1:17

Most people would rather not receive the vision that is held forth in the book of Revelation. It has gained bad press over the centuries as the domain of fanatics and fundamentalists. It is violent and bizarre in several of its passages, and is therefore hard to interpret. "And so are you having nightmares?" a church leader asked me when I told him I was contemplating writing this book.

I was led to examine Revelation by means of an unusual route and believe now that it holds an important place in the mainstream of Christian thinking, presenting a fascinating symbolic profile to believers, inquirers and non-believers alike.

It was refugees that led me to drink of this well. Working with Karen people from Burma who had resettled in Australia from refugee camps in Thailand, I was asked by the church youth in 2010 to lead studies on Revelation. Their request led me for the first time to consider the text of the book seriously. I soon realised that it is a significant part of the bible for them and that they wanted a helpful interpretation of it, being familiar, as they were, with the misinterpretations that are presented by sects like the Jehovah Witnesses.

As I began to delve into commentaries, I soon came across contributions by writers who were reflecting on the book within oppressed situations, having a similar background to the refugees with whom I was working. In particular, I discovered two volumes, one by Allan Boesak, written during the apartheid days of South Africa, and the other by Pablo

Richard, written from within the struggles of Latin American poor communities.[1]

These writers and their communities are able to sit more naturally with the violence of the book, that aspect of Revelation which is a "turn-off" for many western readers. Black communities of South Africa were described as being able to engage and stay with the violent images and to find meaning in them based on what they knew from their own experience. The members of the Base Christian Communities of Latin America are able to read and interpret the catastrophes in the book and gain strength for their faith and struggle. In the West we are largely cocooned from violence; it sits in our experience as a kind of virtual form of reality unless we are exposed to forms of domestic violence or other types of personal abuse. Most of the time it is relegated to the TV screen or to computer games which can be switched off at any moment that we choose.

The standpoint of the oppressed enables us to take hold of a major key to interpret the text. Surprisingly, there is a confrontation with the world and its incessantly violent history that is depicted in the text. The persistence of the righteousness of the Lamb-depicted Christ and his followers, blessed by almighty God, precipitates the CLASH between the world and its history on the one hand and the Lamb and his followers on the other hand.

We cannot switch off this program. The violence of the world is exposed for what it is in its laid-bare reality. As we in the West allow the oppressed and their representatives to come alongside and influence us, then we are obliged to change our thinking, face the horror of violence - the terrifying might of evil. The mysterious nature of evil, we come to realise, is not simply the benign absence of good, but it is an intrinsic force that haunts and has its grip on our world and human beings. The name given to it in the New Testament is "the principalities and powers".

---

1 Boesak, Allan A. *Comfort and Protest, The Apocalypse from a South African Perspective*, Philadelphia, Westminster Press, 1987 and Richard Pablo. *Apocalypse: A People's Commentary on the Book of Revelation*, Eugene, Wipf & Stock, 1995.

Chapter One - Receiving the Vision

John, the writer of Revelation, is led to write to the churches within the colossus and clout of the Roman Empire. He first sees the Christ. He sees Christ standing in the midst of the churches of Asia (later named Asia Minor, present day south-west Turkey) at the time of around 100 CE. He sees in his vision a more heavenly risen Christ than the immediately post-resurrection appearances of the risen Jesus, described in the gospels. John's is a powerful image of the Christ who is both heavenly and present within the communities of faith, having triumphed over sin and evil, beckoning them "to overcome" in the face of emerging persecution.

John sees. He is a seer. We find the words "I saw…." often within the unfolding chapters of Revelation. He sees into the vision and hands it onto those who will receive it in his time and ours, so that then and now we may also see. His vision is to be shared. I have therefore adopted a "reader response" approach to discussing Revelation, indicated by the title of each of the ten chapters in the first section starting with an active "…ing" verb: Receiving, Picturing, Re-awakening… My prayer is that as you, the reader, and I enter into John's written-down vision we may see too, but with a well-considered interpretative lens. It is necessary first to acquire the lens.

The whole vision of John is written down and has become authoritative in the history of the Church. Naturally, we can expect it has also been controversial and misinterpreted. It is a vision, powerfully symbolic in its complex form, prophetic of the present and the future. For the inquirer, it presents itself at first as a crazy vision, verging on the absurd due to its lack of rationality. This character of John's book then becomes the means of perceiving its inspiration, as we enter into the dream-like domain.

Let us be mindful of the basic structure. Strictly speaking, it is not a book but a letter, "written to the seven churches of Asia."

> John introduces himself; he is a prophet
> He conveys the Spirit's message to the churches
> Jesus Christ, the Lamb, is worshipped by God's people

> The seven scrolls, seven trumpets, seven bowls
> The Beasts and Babylon, the Great City
> The Holy City, which descends from heaven.

The title of the book is translated into English, "Revelation", with the original in Greek, "The Apocalypse of John". Both titles mean "unveiling". Images abound in the text. Peppered throughout are scenes of the heavenly worship of God's people and of the amazing image of the marriage feast of the Lamb (3:20, 19:9, 22:21) in which the Lamb is wedded to his Bride.

In this first chapter it is well worthwhile giving a brief background picture of the work of Jesus Christ, that is, the mission that he brought to the world - on the basis of which Christians claim the uniqueness of his work in breaking the bonds of evil. It is also on this basis that Revelation will present powerful, evocative images of him.

Mark presents Jesus at the start of his gospel delivering possessed folk from the demons. As they cry out in defeat the demons name him "the Son of God" (indicating that ready recognition of him occurs in the spiritual realm). Jesus proclaims that the Kingdom of God is at hand and he is seen teaching with authority, cutting through the religious legalism of the day. The crowds see the Kingdom present in his miracles. He adopts voluntary poverty as his lifestyle, teaching his followers to do the same; he is thus free of ties that would restrict his mission. He opens up a sense of God's generosity to sinners and strugglers, which awakens many to want to follow him. He calls God "Father" and teaches the power of forgiveness. Exemplified in the parable of the beggar Lazarus at the rich man's gate, he severely judges the accumulation of wealth. Soon he comes into conflict with the existing national leaders. His death becomes a display of the New Life he offers over against the self-interested, compromising ways of the society. His sacrifice defies and overcomes the principalities and powers. God raises him and the Holy Spirit is given to equip followers to live the New Life in subsequent generations.

Chapter One - Receiving the Vision

This background sketch can provide a sense of why so much is claimed about the historical Jesus as the book of Revelation unfolds.

It is said that Revelation just made it into the canon of scripture. After its inclusion in the fourth century its authority continued to be questioned. Even Martin Luther, the 17th century reformer, doubted its significance.

Looking back over the ups and downs of its interpretation we can legitimately come to the point of saying that it is indeed a part of the collective wisdom of the post-Easter, Spirit-guided community of the Church. However, its interpretation is of key importance and is a matter of high debate today. This volume takes a particular angle and argues for it. In the introduction I have laid out what I believe to be the key tools or lens of interpretation; being equipped with them will help you, the reader, undergo the journey of immersing yourself in the wondrous mysteries of Revelation.

Two avenues, I believe, in our own time contribute a great deal to a holistic view of the book, rescuing it from the grasp of literalists, fundamentalists and those who are determined to misuse it as a source of historical prediction.

The first is that which I have indicated earlier in this chapter. It is the underbelly of the world-wide Christian community, those adherents who number among the oppressed, and who have in recent times brought to bear insight regarding an approach of integrity to the text.

The other source is the tradition of the Orthodox Church, the eastern branch of Christianity, which has evolved an approach to the book that incorporates the apocalyptic imagery into the very centre of the Church's life, her liturgy, symbolism and architecture. Significantly, the Orthodox do not read from the book of Revelation in their liturgies, rather, they seek to make its thrust co-terminus with their worshipping life, as End-connected and End-embraced. I particularly refer to this body of wisdom in chs. 5-7 and 10.

These two avenues will be explored as key interpreters of the text at hand for the early twenty-first century.

Why is it that the oppressed of the world are able genuinely to interpret this book? We have already seen that they are accustomed to violence and are able therefore to see the place of it as it is presented in the clash between the forces of God and of evil. A more central reason is to do with the nature of apocalyptic literature. Swirling dream-like visions emerge in religious communities when people have been forced to have their backs to the wall, having nowhere to move, oppressed to the point of life danger and starvation. They dream of a future given by God. Jewish apocalyptic thought has the perpetrators of evil destroyed at last. The apocalyptic writers see the forces of God coming to bring about the justice that God's servants cannot secure, to begin the reign of heaven on earth.

The Christian communities to which John writes are beginning to experience death-dealing oppression (see Rev2:13). John uses material in his letter strongly leaning on the Hebrews scriptures (the "Old Testament"), such as from the book of Daniel in which babies are killed in front of their mothers because they had them circumcised according to the Law. This horrendous situation can be compared with the background context of Revelation in which believing parents are taken from the children to be tortured or killed.[2]

Oppressed communities use apocalyptic language to uncover the presence of domination and its accompanying ideology. The ideology serves to conceal injustices and legitimize domination. Christian apocalyptic thought, as we see it in the New Testament, un-conceals the world of the poor and legitimises their struggle for the reign of God, which is life and liberation.[3] It does so not in the traditional Jewish way of its apocalyptic genre, by a vengeful battle and victory of the people of God over the people of darkness. Rather, the victory of the reign of God is based on the vision of the cross of Christ, the Lamb, and is understood to be won basically there, with a final unfolding yet to come. John uses and transforms Jewish apocalyptic thought. He leans on passages from Ezekiel, Zechariah and Daniel, as well as themes within the book of

---

[2] See Boring, Eugene M. *Revelation* Louisville: John Knox Press, 1989
[3] Richard, *Apocalypse*.

Exodus.[4] But his apocalyptic vision becomes one anchored in peace and the end of violence - the birth pangs of the new creation. It portrays the followers of the Lamb, not in battle (although often using battle imagery) but bearing witness in service to the loving and forgiving crucified Lord, strongly exposing injustices, until their mission is finally complete.

Hence this type of apocalyptic writing sees Christ at the centre of the believing community, calling, sustaining and blessing, as its redeemer, liberator and Lord. Refugee people like the Karen people know the importance of this apocalyptic vision to comfort and strengthen them in their times of war, killings, rape and torture.[5]

And so it is that John receives the vision. He falls down as though dead at its initiating grandeur (1:17). It is a unique vision, given for that time and for all time. We too are called to receive and enter the vision, to be exposed to the clash and the glory entailed. It is not just for John. It is not just for the seven churches to whom he writes his letter. It is for all who see the need of a genuine deep path of freedom to be embraced, for themselves, for humanity and for the whole creation. " 'Do not be afraid,' says the risen Lord" (1:17).

Probably the most popular example in history of the vision received and lived after John's time comes from the black American period of slavery leading up to 1865. The "negro spirituals" were sung in the plantation "praise houses" and at secret places as apocalyptic longings for the incoming reign of God, and as expressions of hope for freedom in their future on earth. This dual motivation is exemplified in the song, *Swing Low*. Based on a passage in Ezekiel they sang of the heavenly chariot:

> Swing low, sweet chariot coming forth to carry me home ...

---

[4] The seeds of apocalyptic thought in Israel's history emerged out of their seventy year exile in Babylon (6th cent. BC) in which the deep sense of an impossible future gave rise to the conviction of God dealing with the nations and bringing justice by closing the age with the righteous being justified. Israel's apocalyptic thinking then further developed in the 3rd century until the time of Christ, as Israel was successively defeated and overrun.

[5] The defensive fighting of the Karen people in Burma against the totalitarian national government continued from the 1960s to 2012 with the beginning of a peace process, but some outbreaks of fighting are still occurring.

> I looked over Jordan and what did I see,
> Comin' forth to carry me home
> A band of angels coming after me…

The worshipping slaves indeed longed for the final Coming of God. At the same time many urgently saw the need to find a way to freedom in this life, for themselves and their children. Hence many tried to run away to a "free country", that they called "my home" or "Sweet Canaan, the Promised Land". This country was on the northern side of Ohio River, that they called "Jordan". And some songs refer to the Underground Railroad, an organization for helping slaves to run away.

Their dual motivation was interlocked. The prayer of longing for God's final Coming reinforced and strengthened their daring, planning and action for a better future, as risky and dangerous as it was. Apocalyptic vision, when truly received, has the character of empowering believers within the impossible context that they find themselves in.

I conclude this chapter with an insight that arose in preparing for the bible studies with the resettled Karen people among whom I was ministering. As a newcomer to Revelation at that time I looked carefully to find a good understanding of it. I came across a small study guide that sought to introduce people in a simple way to the mysteries of the text. Rev1:3 implies that the whole vision was to be read (aloud) to each of the seven church congregations, maybe in one sitting. The study guide suggested that we can imagine the whole text having been read to a congregation and there is a child sitting in the front, who exclaims at the end of the reading, "isn't it wonderful that the Lamb defeated the Beast!"

There is a converse factor to the familiarity of oppressed groups with violence and their ability to cope with the images presented in Revelation. They have also experienced levels of trauma as result of violence. I was aware of this factor as we began the study series. How was the group of young refugees whom I was teaching going to manage the horrific images that are relayed in the middle chapters? In order to assist in maintaining a sense of the grace-filled core of the book and its assurance of redemption, we began and ended each session by acclaiming together as an antiphon, "Isn't it wonderful that the Lamb defeated the Beast!" It is true to say that "John gives us a message of hope with an unprecedented power."⁶

---

6 Cited in Dorothy Lee, *Hallowed in Truth and Love*, p. 219, quoting Jean-Pierre Prevost, *How to Read Revelation*. In Dr Lee's book she examines the spirituality of Johannine literature, including Revelation.

Chapter Two

Picturing John on Patmos

I, John, your brother and companion...was on the island of Patmos because of the Word of God and the testimony of Jesus. 1:9

Banished to Patmos:
a dry, rocky, wind-swept island,
embracing views in all directions,
with meandering tracks -
a marginal environment
of figs, grapes, oranges, wild tomatoes, goats and donkeys,
then as now;
but then an island of banishment and vision.

The "because of" in the introductory verse to this chapter, gives us the sense that it was the active Word of God and the testimony of Jesus, that is, preaching and evangelism, that were the cause of John being on the island of Patmos. In other words, he was banished to the island by the Roman authorities. This conclusion fits with the evidence of persecution being instigated at that time, namely, about 95 CE.

Eusebius, the "father of church history", writing in the early fourth century, reports that John was released from Patmos under the emperor Domitian's successor, Nerva (96-98). It is therefore estimated that John stayed on the island about eighteen months.

I visited Patmos during the process of writing this book. The islands in this part of the Aegean Sea are dry and rocky, with Patmos being not far from the south-east coast of Turkey. Many tourists, travellers and pilgrims visit the island each year. A major feature is the Cave of Apocalypsis which is dedicated to the receiving of the vision by John. Pilgrims pray there, travellers note it and tourists walk in and out unaffected... Situated above, on a high hill stands the grand eleventh century monastery. From the cave I looked out across the island and the

Aegean towards the coast of what in John's time was called Asia: a sight that could lend itself to having a heavenly vision.

"But was John psychotic?" it has been asked, "after all, the vision that he has is wild in the extreme!" A central characteristic of apocalyptic thought involves cataclysms of cosmic drama bringing in the end of the world, and so it could be said that the apocalyptic genre may lend itself to the possibility of manic imagination. The tell-tale that this suggestion is not the case lies in the fact that John's consequent letter is written with a deep knowledge of the Hebrew scriptures. He uses them to present an incredibly profound, albeit complex, picture of the end times. He is clearly a scholar and a meditator of God's Word. He is richly familiar with the Jewish heritage and also he is a crafter of the emerging Christian tradition.

Whilst John might not be what today we would in any way label mentally ill, there is what I would like to call a kind of "wild holiness" about him and his writing, a form of almost extreme, left-field wisdom to convey the mystery of God's purpose in the present, oriented towards the future. (A good example is that of the four housemen in Rev6, to be discussed in chapter four.) Wild holiness is needed in the religious endeavor in order to cut across strongly maintained positions that often narrow down to obsession or exclusiveness. We are not entertaining here those presentations of a fundamentalist apocalyptic focus which in themselves are overly narrow, but rather, wise words and illustrations that pull us up from the narrowing path we may be going down. Wild holiness is radically open to the Spirit and at the same time passionately concerned for people, as John was for the seven churches.

The refugee situation that I have been involved with for twelve years has further alerted me to the apocalyptic approach as "wild holiness". My first visit to the largest of the Karen camps on the Thai Burma border involved a memorable incident along these lines. I was with an Australian group attending a meeting at which Karen church members were welcoming us. While a series of courteous speeches were being presented suddenly an old refugee with a white beard stood up and with a powerful projection in his voice interrupted the speaker and like a fiery preacher announced, "Christ is coming, he is coming very soon and we'll be rescued from this imprisonment." Fortunately, as this exclamation was uttered in the Karen language I had beside me an able translator so that I was able to savor the moment.

This incident will be reminiscent to older readers of those city street corner preachers, often with beards, who decades ago wore billboards over the shoulders with the words, "The End is near." There seemed to be at least one of these characters in every western city.

But the character, whom in my mind I had named "Moses", rose up in a refugee context. His proclamation appeared to hold more credibility than one given on a city corner in the West, rendering, I felt, a valid instance of wild holiness, alerting us to the validity of this way of thinking and believing.

John, writing in the apocalyptic genre, indicates that the End is coming soon (1:3). What does he mean by it? I shall explore this topic later in this chapter.

In the meantime it is worth noticing that the felt authenticity of the utterance by "Moses" lies in the fact that refugees who are incarcerated for many years daily feel like wounded birds in a small cage. My visit was in 2000. The refugee camp opened in 1985 and he had lived in these conditions since then. He was a devout lay leader with a family of twelve children. Apocalyptic thinking arises powerfully out of imprisoned circumstances, when there is nowhere else to turn for freedom except to call on the Lord pleadingly to come: "Come, Lord, come."

The apocalyptic genre therefore is that way of thinking and believing that is most powerfully entered into when you are cornered, as we noted in chapter one. Its speakers and writers function in the world and Church today as those who maintain a clarion call to the rest of us.

Let us return to John's particular historical circumstance. What was the situation of the generation of Christians of which he was a part? His letter indicates that persecution has already begun. The verse 1:9, with which this chapter begins, includes the words (here in italics): "I, John, your brother and companion *in the suffering and the kingdom and patient endurance that are ours in Jesus* was on the island...." Pablo Richard makes the point that prophets had a strong role in the churches of Revelation. As their brother and companion John shares in these three characteristics of suffering, the kingdom and patient endurance. However, these characteristics, Richard argues, are more accurately translated, *distress, reign and resistance.*[1] Appreciating what his fellow Christians were going through, this latter group of words conveys a sharper shared experience and can provide us with a clearer sense of what was taking place and how they felt.

John feels the weight of their "distress" as he thinks and prays on Patmos for the congregations, distress due to the threats of persecution, of their marginalisation and humiliation under the Roman yoke. He shares in God's "reign", as they seek to witness to Christ's Kingdom on earth and he supports their active "resistance" to the destructive powers around them.

John's knowledge of their situation is accompanied by his familiarity with the temple in Jerusalem and Israel's history. In all probability he, a Jewish Christian, was one of the many who fled from Palestine after the destruction of the temple in 70 CE. Jews and Christians alike settled in Asia.

At that time the empire was troubled by wars. The tyranny and death in 68 CE of Nero had not been followed by a time of stability but by further wars and by three emperors in two years. Earthquakes had devastated the region of Asia in the sixties.

The Christians who settled in Asia at the end of the first century were considered a sect, a suspect group of adherents who were mainly from the lower classes. Meeting on a day (Sunday) that was not a public holiday, the Christians were regarded as suspect and unpatriotic. What

---

[1] p.50 in Richard; his own footnote explains that the word usually given as 'endurance', in Greek, is better translated 'resistance' since the noun is an active stance, implying engagement in history.

were their so-called "love-feasts"? Due to their meetings being in homes these feasts were at times likened to orgies. Did the "body and blood of Christ" that they consumed mean that they were cannibals? Rumours grew. Furthermore, why was their leader crucified as a criminal in Judea?

The followers of Jesus of Nazareth, now some 60 years after his death, were seen as disloyal to the emperor, sometimes being labelled "atheists" due to their refusal to bow and make offerings at the shrine of the emperor.

Hence, at that time the Christians were becoming subject to economic and social discrimination including harassment and plundering of property (Hebrews 10:34, 12:4, I Peter 4:14f).

The Jewish communities, who also came into Asia, were not so badly discriminated against. They had a continuing long and stable presence in the empire and had made an agreement with the authorities in which they pledged to pray for the divinely acclaimed emperor and not to him.

As the Christian communities were increasingly becoming Gentile in membership issues of identity were being posed by themselves, "Who are we as God's people in this different situation?" John writes to address this question.

Significantly, the cult of the emperor had developed from the reign of Caesar (44 BC). At his death a comet was seen in the sky; "Caesar has gone to God", witnesses proclaimed. His son, Augustus, campaigned to become recognised as the "Son of God" who will bring unity, peace and prosperity to the world. Hymns were written to him announcing his "eternal reign" – "there is no name but Augustus by which man can be saved."

As the cult of the emperor developed Domitian (81-96 CE) had a statue of solid gold erected, depicting him holding a scroll. As he travelled around the cities of the empire twenty-four singers went before him in procession. He loved to watch death and destruction. When a priest offended him he had the priest burnt alive.

Some scholars say that Domitian was the first emperor to understand the Christian movement as a threat. John will write – in Rev4 – "I was in heaven and there was a throne, with one seated on the throne." The vision expands to include the twenty-four elders (representing the completed covenants of God with humanity). The scene is that of a universal king and it is not Domitian. The *Pax Romanum* under the emperors had taken further steps to maintain its force-based "peace".[2] John will write messages to the churches that convey, "Whatever you do as Christians, do not bow down to the emperor or offer the required sacrifices to him, even though you are hearing of your fellow Christians being killed" (see Rev 2:13).

The churches in Asia are now in a far different situation from the Church of the apostles in Palestine; even different from the churches to whom St Paul writes. How can disciples of Jesus be obedient to their Lord in these new circumstances? John's letter is directed to these Christians, cognizant of the demands placed upon them.

So, who is this John? Traditionally, he has been understood as the same person as the writer of the fourth gospel, John the Elder, with links to the apostle, John. If the apostle had been the writer of Revelation he would have been extremely old in 96 CE, the estimated date of writing. But the John of Revelation presents himself as a prophet (1:3). Most modern-day scholars take the position that he is not the same person as the writer of the Gospel of John or of the Johannine letters, due to the differences of language and theology. At the same time there are thematic similarities to the gospel. Some scholars therefore regard the prophet John to be part of a Johannine circle that was centred in Ephesus and is the means by which there is a form of continuity in the writing of each of the "Johannine" books, with roots back to the apostle himself.[3]

---

[2] Walter Wink summaries the *Pax Romanum* as follows: The Roman Empire had brought peace to a fracticidal world. It presided over a period of unparalleled prosperity (for the prosperous). Its might was so legendary that a single emissary could prompt surrender. But this façade of magnificence was brought at a horrible price. The revelation that comes to John strips off the mask of benevolence and reveals beneath it the true spirit of Rome. *Engaging the Powers*, p. 89.

Did John of the Apocaplyse believe that the End would be soon in the historical, chronological sense? "Blessed are those who read the words of this prophecy ... because the time is near?" (1:3). He may have well believed this. There are indications in St Paul's early writings (1&2 Thessal.) that he believed the final coming would happen in his lifetime. He widens his understanding in his later letters. The topic of a delay is not a problem for Paul. Furthermore, there are indications in the gospels that Jesus himself believed the End was near. However, he also taught, "Not even the Son knows the day or the hour" (Mark 13:32).

John, in fact, does not present a simply chronological kind of "soonness". Rather, he emphasizes, along with the cosmic events in their symbolic meaning, a vision of grace and salvation in the present. He focuses on worship and discipleship now in the face of the coming events. Indeed, the cataclysmic events have already begun, but not in a chronological order, since it is a symbolic portrayal in which the events represent and point to deeper realities.

The text of his letter resists any date-setting regarding the future and utilises numerology to symbolize the meaning of things (see ch.5). The date-setting obsession of fundamentalists is a concern that sometimes can attract vulnerable or less educated Christians. In the first chapter I indicated how Karen refugees in 2010 invited me to take an interest in Revelation. The trigger that led them to ask me to start a study series on the book was the movie *2012*, which they had just seen. It was a standard culturally apocalyptic-styled movie of cities being destroyed and people trying to escape disaster. The Karen people had not been exposed to movies of this type. "Is it true?" they asked. "No," I promptly replied, "the movie is about Hollywood wanting to make a lot of money..."

The expectation that is awakened by "soonness", "the End is near", is not simply chronological. However, the sense of tip-toe expectation in relation to "what is about to happen" lies at the heart of being a Christian. It breeds alertness due to the bestowal of the Holy Spirit at Pentecost

---

3 John is envisaged on Patmos with icons and frescoes of him depicting him as elderly; he is devoutly referred to as St John the Theologian.

following the events of Good Friday and Easter. The Spirit's activity is the down-payment[4] that leads to the End.

Alertness is the attitude or orientation of those who endure faithfully. The endurance is not a dull, resigned and disempowered waiting but, rather, is sustained by resistance, building demonstrations of the coming Kingdom in the present at the same time as participating in the spiritual dynamism of worship and the heavenly vision. According to this understanding, believers do not see themselves as positioned at a large distance from the realities of the End-time. John writes in such a way as to anchor our alertness with access to the heavenly choir and its praise, and, to fellowship with the martyrs and saints who await the Final Day and are now at the Gate of Heaven.

Soonness, therefore, is a spiritual category in which expectation, alertness, worship and heavenly connection are already at hand. In this sense the New Testament refers to "the Last Days". Peter, in his sermon at Pentecost (Acts 2) proclaims that the Last Days have begun with the outpouring of the Spirit; it is the fulfilment of the prophecy of Joel. If we are indeed living in the period of the Last Days, the time leading to the End, then these qualities of soonness are central to the life of faith now.

John writes to people facing tribulation: "endure, the End is near." Maintaining the alertness of faith will strengthen their endurance. They will live in the power of the Spirit. God will bring all that he has made to its fulfillment. John on Patmos has his heart turned to the plight of the believers in his generation, to struggling believers who find themselves embedded in the mighty machine of the Roman Empire. He invites them to be embraced by the vision given to him, "in the Spirit ..., on the Lord's Day."

---

4 Hendrikus Berkoff. *The Christian Faith* Michigan: Eerdmans, 1985.

Chapter Three

Re-Awakening to Christ in the Midst

I turned and saw among the lampstands someone "like a son of man." 1:13

"Mystical" is a word that is necessary in thinking about apocalyptic literature, including the book of Revelation. The text Rev1:13 (above) presents itself as immediately mystical. The word is difficult to define. Indicating a dimension of human experience, it conveys a deeply spiritual sense, beyond the normal parameters of this world, yet occurring at times in the course of daily life. When it is used in relation to apocalytic literature it speaks of an "unveiling" (literal meaning of apocalyptic), a revealing of things heavenly, unseen. And so Christian mysticism can be defined as knowledge of God's grace in Christ in ways that are beyond the rational.

It is important to say a little further in relation to the topic of the "mystical." If God and the Kingdom of God are transcendent realities, they are *apprehended*, not comprehended. Apprehension involves only partial rational understanding - a going beyond - whereas comprehension normally involves a rational grasping of the subject. In apprehension we advance in knowledge of the subject, at least in part, mystically. For Christians this 'advancing' takes place in personal and communal ways, especially in prayer and worship.

In writing to the churches – Rev2&3 - John is caught up in mystical experience. Firstly, he sees the risen Christ standing among the seven churches to whom he is told to write (1:12-20). John's vision is *for* the churches. At the same time we can ask, "does the vision relate to following generations of the Church, including our own?" The clue here is the number seven. Numbers in his letter have symbolic meaning. Seven indicates completeness and so the messages to the churches can be said to cover the span of the ways in which churches live and have faith; here is a whole message that is universal in its relevance. The messages to the seven churches are relevant now as much as then.

Let us look at the vision of Christ that John saw. "I saw one like a Son of Man clothed with a long robe" (1:13). Here John is adopting an image from the apocalyptic book of Daniel which was hugely popular with the Jewish people in the first century. The heavenly one who will come at the end of time wears "a gold sash around his chest" (as a high priest)… "his head and hair are as white as wool" (indicating dignity and wisdom) … "his eyes are like burning fire" (meaning penetrating insight) …. "and his face is like the sun shining in all its brilliance" (he is Lord of all).

> *Pictured opposite, this icon of the apocalyptic Christ can be seen on Patmos and neighbouring islands. Jesus Christ is sitting on an arch of angels with dark wings; similar angels are seen at the top of the icon, becoming purified. The Christ's wounds are healed. The seven stars are in his right hand. The sword has come from his mouth. There is a sense of wisdom and forbearance in the face of Christ. The substantial depiction of St John at the bottom of the icon presents him lying with his head resting on a heavenly cloud. He appears peaceful as he apprehends the great vision.*

John's vision of the risen Lord is different from the post-Easter appearances in the gospels. In the gospels usually the disciples recognise Jesus - he brings them a message but his appearance is not described. Here in Rev1 his heavenly appearance is visibly described, accommodated to the situation at hand, encouraging and exhorting the seven churches, "I am the first and the last…" (v.17f).

In this vision Christ stands among "the lampstands", which represent the churches. He holds "the keys of Death and Hades"[1] (v.18) and he commands John to "write what you have seen, what is now and what is to take place" (v.19).

The first point to note in relation to the messages to the churches is the presence of an angel in each. John is instructed, "To the angel in the church … write…" An angel is identified with each church. Yet, it is to be noted that the basic understanding of who or what angels are, is as messengers – those beings who bring messages from heaven to earth.

---

1 'Hades' is the underworld, not 'hell', see ch. 9.

Chapter Three - Re-Awakening to Christ in the Midst

The Revelation - St. John's Vision of Christ and the seven Candlesticks Icon in the Treasury Museum at the Monastery of St John, in Patmos, Greece - photo ©Randa Bishop

However, an ancient Jewish tradition about angels is introduced here, which is present in other parts of Revelation, namely, a belief that God's sphere of being and operation, heaven, and our sphere, earth, are not actually separated by a great gulf. They meet and merge and meld into one another in all kinds of ways. A (heavenly) angel is envisaged as immersed in the communal life of a particular church, representing its character, adhering, even identifying with the strengths and weaknesses of the congregation in the totality of that local church's life.[2] It appears that the angels have become a little "dark" due to their immersion in the churches and the all-too-human factors involved[3].

At once, we are confronted with a mystical sense of "church", both as the called-out body of believers and as the community that moves forward in some direct connection with the heavenly reality; this connection is brought about by virtue of the grace of Jesus Christ, the robed Son of Man who stands in the midst of the churches.

The messages from the living Lord are mediated to John by the Holy Spirit, to be passed onto the churches. On the basis of the angelic presence in each of the churches, it is not possible to reduce the identity of "church" to a visible or tightly logical category, whether in John's time, in subsequent generations or in our own. Churches cannot be reduced to a simply human category of a group of believers with measurable strengths and weaknesses. This insight is poignant in terms of understanding what a church is at any point of time and in any place – it is a profoundly spiritual entity. As we look around the congregation on Sundays in our own time there is more at hand than what we see with the physical eye.

To each of the churches the message exhorts the people "to overcome" (which includes "to resist") in the face of tribulation. He writes to Ephesus, Smyrna, Pergamum, Thyatira, Sardis, Philadelphia and Laodicea. Each church has its own particular point of spiritual weakness; they are harassed

---

[2] For a further discussion in this topic see Wink, Walter. *Unmasking the Powers*. P. 69f..
[3] Revelation holds a significant place for dark or fallen angels – see Rev 9:13f.

by evil forces from within and from without. In Ephesus "they had lost their first love" (2:4); in Laodicea "they are neither hot nor cold" (3:15).

The weaknesses in the churches are due largely to the fact that they must face tribulation. The thrust here is of great relevance to the churches today that face persecution or face glaringly difficult obstacles, such as large-scale poverty. Persecution, or oppression in various forms, is commonly linked to poverty and hence to having enemies who are close at hand. The churches who do not suffer these threats directly nevertheless are called to live in solidarity with them, particularly in a globalized world.

The Peruvian theologian, Gustav Gutierrez, has pointed out that to be a Christian you must have enemies and you are called to love them. Love is the basic standpoint of churches and to have enemies whom you love. If churches today in the West say that they have no enemies, what does this say about their witness? Where is their solidarity? Are they neither hot nor cold, like the Laodiceans? Can a keen form of resistance be seen?

The tribulation that is facing the churches is referred to soon after the writing of Revelation in another source. Eugene Boring, in his excellent commentary on Revelation, sets out the evidence regarding the plight of the Christians soon after the reign of Domitian, recorded in Pliny's[4] letter to the emperor, Trajan, written about 112 CE.

> Pliny's letter pictures the kind of event that was happening in John's time… Christians are brought to the Roman magistrate… and are required to say "Caesar is Lord", an exact counterpart of the basic Christian confession "Jesus is Lord" (Rom 10:9…). In addition, they were required to curse Christ.[5]

Domitian decreed that all imperial proclamations must begin, "Our Lord and God Domitian commands…." It was reported that he had many people, including Christians, executed for "atheism", that is, failure to worship the gods of Rome, of whom he was one.[6]

---

4 Pliny (the Younger) was Governor of Bithynia within the Roman empire.
5 Eugene M Boring. *Revelation* Louisville: John Knox Press, 1989..
6 Dio Cassius, *Roman History* 67:14.

Christians in today's world face similar life and death obstacles. No longer can any churches, regardless of location, avoid the presence of tribulation and the exhortation to endure. More than ever, in an age of instant global communication, we are made aware in the West of the plight of Christians who are struggling for their lives. Migrant and refugee congregations are springing up more and more in the suburbs and towns of developed countries, carrying with them deep wounds. The issues of injustice, whether in our own country, or overseas, become matters of significance for us as we realise again that they are genuinely our brothers and sisters.

Pictured on a large scale in Rev6-20 the conflicts are already at hand, within and bearing down from outside upon the churches. The churches are not spectators in the ensuing cosmic battle between the agents of God and the forces of evil, but they experience this battle in their own lives as believers, individually and communally.

Karen refugee Christians, whether they have resettled to the West, remain in Thailand or reside in Burma, will rarely speak openly of this struggle as they have been exposed to it, but they know it in their bones. Are we sufficiently familiar in the churches of the West with the realities of the struggle with the forces of evil, within and without? John's messages to the seven churches display a tight nexus between the vision of the risen Lord in their midst - to which they and we must become re-awakened - and the plight of faithful believing and witnessing disciples in a grossly unjust world. To live within this vision is knocking on the doors of the western churches, to be known and lived.

Distinctive qualities are appealed to in John's seven messages. Two qualities that particularly stand out are *repentance* and *holding firm*. As the messages imply, these must always be alive and well within the pulse of church life, as aspects of the fervor and ferment of the Faith.

Some historians point out that the church in the large and beautiful city of Ephesus[7] grew very strong in the second century and by the end of

---

[7] Ephesus today is a magnificent ruin, visited by many tourists but usually not mentioned on modern maps of Turkey.

Chapter Three - Re-Awakening to Christ in the Midst

the third century many of its members had spread to other cities in the region. By the end of the fourth century Christianity was present in all parts of the empire.

The seeds of faithfulness and growth that John passionately believed in, involves presenting challenges-in-hope. The Lord Christ overarches and abides faithfully in the churches, "his face shining like the sun", beckoning followers in every generation not to bow down to the idols in the surrounding culture and its dominating forms of authority. Obedience is to the true king, who now is at the right hand of the Almighty with our relationship to heaven being close, dynamic and infused.

With his opening apocalytic picture John will soon shift his image of the risen Christ standing among the churches to that of the Lion and the sacrificial Lamb in heaven, as we progress with him in his vision.

Chapter Four

Facing Systemic Evil

The Lamb opens the scroll. 6:1

In this chapter we shall contemplate some grand themes and forceful images. Firstly, there is the appearing of the Lamb in John's vision. Then we shall look at what is meant by "facing systemic evil". Finally, we shall briefly provide an overview of the three "sevens": the scrolls, the trumpets and the bowls that present the beginning of God's judgment, themes that make up the bulk of the middle section of John's vision (chs. 6-11).

The appearing of the Lamb

In Rev5 a question is posed in heaven about the scroll. "Who is worthy to open it?" Only the Lion of Judah who then becomes the Lamb is worthy (vv.5-6). He is worthy because he has brought about the change, the break in the cycle of universal destruction and violence. Mentioned twenty-eight times in Revelation, Christ is imaged as the Lamb - slain, immolated, and now in heaven; here is one of the great characteristic ideas of the whole text.

The lambs of sacrifice prescribed in the Law of Moses were offered each year at the Passover. The moon was full as the people, having come up to Jerusalem, offered a lamb, family by family, in the Temple where it was sacrificed by the priests. The reason they did this ritual was to recall God's liberation of the people from slavery in Egypt and to renew their covenant with God. Now there is a new lamb, the Lamb of the New Covenant, the unique, once-for-all Lamb.

Interestingly, as Boesak points out[1], John changes the word for "lamb" in its common biblical usage to a more specific term, that of a young ram[2].

---
1 In his book, *Comfort and Protest*.
2 *Amnos* is the word used usually for Lamb but here *arnion* is used, only cited elsewhere

The change presumably indicates a strong sense of "lamb", one who is able to lead the flock, even up steep, dry hills. The flock will be the followers of the Lamb in every generation. Jesus is therefore seen as forging his non-violent, peace-filled passage of transforming the locked-in old system of death-dealing and destruction into the New Life and freedom of God's Reign. This work of Christ reaches its climax on the cross. The resurrection of Jesus from the dead by God is the trans-historical sign that the Reign of God through his Son on earth is dawning.

The Gospel of John describes the confrontation between the way of the destructive world with its rulers and the way of Jesus when he stands before Pontius Pilate at his trial on the day of his death: "My kingdom is not of this world, if it were ... my followers would take up arms and fight..." (John 18:36).

John, the seer, here holds his vision within the post-Easter period, the time between the resurrection and the End. The image of the Lamb as victor is central. It is presented in contrast to other images that the Hebrew Testament presents of the victor: the warrior God or King (e.g. David). The Lamb, although seemingly weak, will be victorious and is already, according to the new foundation established by the cross and resurrection, winning the "battle". He now reigns in heaven and we ourselves can see him, actively reigning, as we become privy to John's vision.

Facing the evils

Disease, war, famine and death have ravaged humanity since the beginning. The opening scene of Rev6 sets forth the widely historical drama in which these forces of destruction are seen to be active in full measure. Starting at verse two, the four horsemen sweep across the stage of the world wreaking havoc: displaying and fully exposing the terrible realities of what human beings do to each other: the white horse

---

in scripture in Jeremiah 11:19.. Rev5:6 portrays the Lamb (*arnion*) of the Apocalypse as "having the marks of having being slain": the sacrifice of Christ is visible in the heavenly places, and, "having seven horns and seven eyes": he possesses wisdom and honor.

– conquest, the red horse – strife, the black horse – famine (set beside luxury) and the pale green horse – pestilence and death.

Developing a deeper consciousness regarding the inhumanity that "man can do to man" has been an arena that I have been catapulted into during the past twelve years. To encounter squarely the plight of refugees, their affliction due to the machine of corrupt government, as it has been in Burma from 1962 to 2012, has indeed been a lesson for me as a westerner. (The future of the democracy in Burma/Myanmar remains uncertain at the time of writing this book.) I had to learn first-hand what the New Testament labels "the principalities and powers" (Ephes.1:2, 3:10, 6:12; Colos.1:6, 2:15) - the spiritual, darkened powers that impinge and effect human beings and the course of history. Walter Wink is a seminal scholar in this topic at hand.[3] He remarks that a precise naming of the powers that assail us is itself a part of the social struggle at hand.

The powers hold their sway in political systems, hence we say that the evil is systemic.[4] Those who lead and rule violent regimes, have become caught up in them and perpetrate massively destructive deeds can be called "hurters:"

> Hurters often seek
> to be better hurters
> they get on a roll
> sadly
> tragically
> for them
> cruelty becomes commonplace.[5]

---

[3] Of Wink's writings, the book that is mostly utilized here is *Engaging the Powers* Mineapolis: Fortress, 1992.
[4] What is basically meant by 'systemic' here is that evil permeates a society. It is active throughout 'the system'. Furthermore, its influence carries over from one generation to the next in the society (see Exod 20:5).
[5] From a collection of poems by the author, *Flickering Lights*, Ginnenderra Press, 2012. The poems trace the Karen refugee journey.

The depiction of the four horsemen is vivid with the variously coloured horses, portrayed in a gallop, the latter three waging wreckage and destruction. The first horse, however, is white; he will conquer – he wears a victor's crown and he holds a bow. A major interpretation is that he is the same white rider that appears in 19:11f. He is the Christ and his bow is the Word of God. The past-present habit and force of destruction by humanity of humanity has been intercepted. Jesus Christ has lived, died and risen. He has cut across and now comes alongside these forces to overcome them.

At least this is one interpretation of the text at this point! Engaging in the task of interpreting the text here, as in other parts of Revelation, we find that the meaning may well be polyvalent (having more than one meaning). What I have just given as an interpretation is based on a classical rendering. But some modern scholars argue that the white horse represents the Parthians who were threatening the eastern borders of the Roman Empire. The Parthians attacked with white horses and so the horsemen, all four, represent the forces of human destructiveness. There is no need according to this interpretation to identify the white horseman with the (other) white horseman in Rev19. The polyvalent nature of the text is understood in a similar way to what happens in the psyche with dreaming – there can be more than one meaning to parts of the dream at the same time. We can appreciate both interpretations.

The main point here regarding the four horsemen is the exposure and full display of the extent of the brutality that humans can engage in, not once, but recurringly. Two depictions come to my mind in relation to this point: one in the form of a description of the last century and the other in the form of art.

In 1994 the philosopher Isaiah Berlin gave "A Message to the 21st Century" at the University of Toronto. It began with these words, remarking on the shocking and unimaginable death toll through wars, military and civilian, in the twentieth century (est. 203 million)[6]:

---

6 Cited in The New York Review of Books, August 2014. In continuing his speech Berlin held out a great hope for the 21st century – "Liberal democracy ... is spreading. Great tyrannies are in ruins ... I feel sure that a better time for mankind is ahead in the 21ist

"It was the best of times and the worst of times." With these words Charles Dickens began his famous novel *A Tale of Two Cities*. But this cannot be said, alas, about our own terrible century. Men have for millennia destroyed each other, but the deeds of Attila the Hun, Genghis Khan, Napoleon (who introduced mass killings in war), even the Armenian massacres pale into insignificance before the Russian Revolution and its aftermath: the oppression, torture, murder which can be laid at the doors of Lenin, Stalin, Hitler, Mao, Pol Pot and the systematic falsification of information which prevented knowledge of these horrors for years – these are unparalleled.

We tend to forget these realities, for as T.S. Eliot remarked, "humankind cannot bear very much reality." Forgetfulness is a major reason why humans do not more forcefully attempt to overcome these evil and why therefore there is the "galloping", shocking presentation of the four horsemen.

Probably the artist in the West who has most exposed the horrors of war is Goya. In his drawings of the Napoleonic Wars his intention was not to spare us, the viewer of his work, regarding what the horrors of war entail. This drawing is entitled "To bury and to shut up" (1863). In his biography, *Goya*, Robert Hughes comments, "the daring of this image can perhaps be assessed by the fact that a century later, during World War II, neither the British nor German censors permitted a newspaper to publish a photo of a corpse." (p. 297).

---

century." He was not to know what political horrors were to occur even early in this century.

foundation of international relations. The Dragon has embodied itself in one empire after another (Dan. 7-8, 11-12). This understanding puts the lie to the vain belief that the violent overthrow of empire will solve the problem created by empire.

Where does the Dragon get these powers? God has permitted it in the handing over that has been done by a humanity derelict of responsibility – see Mark 13.[12] An empire as a system, although not preeminently chaotic, is nevertheless in a permanent crisis of legitimation and it is held together by force. Propaganda is essential to its continuance in order to delude humanity into a level of stupefaction.

The cosmic clash

The deconstruction of the Domination System has begun. The gallop of the four horsemen displays that which must now be broken down. John sees the three symbols of the scroll, the trumpets and the bowls as announcing this process taking place. The scroll is proclaimed, the trumpets sound and the bowls are poured forth. All three were used in Jewish worship, with the first two used to indicate proclamation and victory, and the bowls to indicate what is required by God's justice to renew communion between God and his people. Here is a kind of apocalyptic liturgy.

As we have seen, the four horsemen are described in the opening of four seals of the scroll. At the end of "the seals" and "the trumpets" there is a window in each of these "sevens" to show the reader the already present activity of worship in heaven. These are intended to encourage the servants of the Lamb as they witness to the Kingdom. At the opening of the sixth seal we see a great earthquake: with this announcement the universal deconstruction has begun. It is symbolically portrayed: "the sun turns black...", "the moon turns blood red" ... and "the sky recedes like a scroll...". These transcendental mythological symbols are used as evocations that the System is coming to its termination.

---

[12] In Mark 13:13: "(The End) will be like a man who has gone away on a journey and leaves his servants in charge, each with his own work and has ordered the door-keeper to stay awake."

Two forms of the cataclysm or catastrophe are present in Revelation (as the introduction mentions). Firstly, there are the catastrophes that represent the destructive forces that have been happening in the course of history - past and present (the four horsemen). They are not telling us what is about to happen in the future (of our history). Yet, they will continue into the future and intensify. They now reveal that God will bring such forces to an end and when we see them occurring we will remember that the End is "near".

The second meaning of the catastrophes is that they represent the now inaugurated clash between the forces of God and of evil, a clash that derives from the decision of God, based on the victory of the Lamb, finally to defeat the evil forces and culminate history. The clash contains violenct acts but due to them being symbolic they do not actually display a God punishing humanity. Tragically, humanity punishes itself. God loves the Creation, as the cross of Christ displays, and will bring it to its completion, with mercy and justice.

Rev6-11 therefore symbolically represents the post-resurrection period as the clash between the agents of God, the Lamb and his followers, with the forces of darkness, the Domination System. Jesus is the new Lord of history. The route to the End is Jesus' way of peace, of the Beatitudes: blessed are the poor in spirit, the mourners, the gentle, those who hunger and thirst for righteousness, the merciful, the pure in heart, the peace-makers and the persecuted for righteousness (Matt 5:1-10).

The manner of interpretation is critically important at this point. How can we understand the reason for John's choice of violent imagery to portray the clash between the forces of God and the forces of Satan?

He adopts traditional apocalyptic language and re-interprets it in a Christian way. To understand his interpretive lens more clearly we must return to the context in which John and the seven churches found themselves. John presents a message of hope in what appears to be impossible circumstances. How can the weak and small congregations survive and be faithful under the mighty weight of Rome? Hope is expressed, and summoned, in terms of apocalyptic violence. It is a writing that is of provocation and defiance.[13] Violence is the classical milieu of apocalyptic writing - the manner of presenting the struggle between good and evil. But thrown into this milieu is the Christian amendment to the apocalyptic genre, namely, the way of the nonviolent Lamb to bring about the deconstruction and reconstruction.

"The retribution of the Lamb" (Rev6:16) is imagery that indicates the divinely bestowed power of the Lamb in his non-violent ministry (in the course of our present history) to defy and overcome the dark powers. John's hearers in the churches are therefore strengthened in their lives and witness. Even as subjected to Roman rule, they have been brought under God's rule of his Son, a rule of peace-making and love, which will triumph. The churches have to face the claim of the empire, *the Pax Romanum*, that was the custodian of greater prosperity and order (compared to the disordered and also cruel societies before it) in all its dominions, but at what cost. The empire became more power-centred, corrupt and demonic as the first century progressed.

Hope in Revelation has nothing to do with moderation. Mediocre consolation - wishy-washy pastoral care - cannot be a substitute for a rigorously conceived hope. As we have seen, Christian hope is most poignantly expressed when all human hoping is blocked. It is a refugee-, incarceration-shaped form of hope that knows daily of trauma, violence and powerlessness. It is hope of adults clinging to the promises of God for a better life for their children. The vision of a better world is to be faithfully adhered to by living the way of Jesus. And "hope against hope" is open to visions.

In Rev8-11 the seven trumpets sound. They are alert signals. There are terrible plagues, reminiscent of the plagues in Egypt that preceded Israel's exodus. The plague imagery is transposed into a mythological, transcendent key and projected onto the cosmic screen. Just as the

---

13 Jacques Ellul. *Apocalypse: The Book of Revelation* New York: Seabury, 1979.

Chapter Four - Facing Systemic Evil

Egyptian oppressors are struck within history, so too all oppressive worldly powers are judged as history itself is brought to an end.[14]

The world itself has been corrupted by the assault of the powers and human collusion with them (sin) so that the divine judgment is comprehensive – of humans, the land, sea and rivers and heavenly bodies.

John is presenting **the intensification** of his visionary narrative: the clash between the forces of God and the forces of evil intensify. We are reminded again not to interpret the text literally. Previous generations often read the events described literally and saw plagues in history, e.g. in the fourteenth century in Europe, as predicting the End. Instead, we are invited to peer into the imagery and move beyond it to the key interpretation – of the certainty of the divine judgment and the fixity of the purposes of the Lamb and his victory.

Interestingly, Christ is not mentioned in the cosmic drama here. Yet the scene is fundamentally about his overcoming of the powers, already having broken them in his time on earth. Christ's breaking of the powers are of cosmic proportions - the earthquake as Jesus died on the cross (Matt 27:51).

Mythological language is necessary therefore to get to grips with the fundamental message of John's vision about God, creation and evil. It is important to maintain the belief throughout the reading of the whole text that the divine will is to save. Do not read Revelation outside the perspective of the perfect, absolute and unbreakable association of Christ and humans.[15]

The bowls of wrath (ch. 15-16) continue the intensification of the clashing vision. The bowls are golden to resemble the bronze basins used by the priests of Israel in the sacrificial rituals. The symbolic character of the vision – corpses, scorching fire on earth, etc. – show forth the forging of God's justice and resolve. The hailstones indicate judgment upon

---

14 See Boring, *Revelation*.
15 Ellul, *Apocalypse*.

humanity in mingling its activities with the evil forces and becoming permeated by them as the dark hidden forces have become lodged in the human psyche and decision-making.

These and other images draw readers into a deeper knowledge of God's purposes. There is a clear hint of **warning** to the Church which in each generation receives the apocalyptic text. Here is a stark appeal towards repentance and to stand erect, to stretch out in courage to the Lamb and be sacrificial witnesses as members of his community.

In the baptismal vows of mainstream churches there is the question, "Do you renounce evil?" or "Will you resist evil?" Evil for Christians is far more than the esoteric, such as occult practices. Its manifestations may include these but the focus in the New Testament is largely on the personal, social and political forms of dark forces. Our preparedness and action to renounce and resist ... must be a part of our Christian living, as we find ourselves pitched within the clash between the forces of the Kingdom of God and of darkness. We are asked to see ourselves as participating in **the ripening** (Berkoff) - like the wheat and tares in the parable of Jesus (Matt 13:25f) - growing towards the Great Harvest and the separation, *krisis* (Greek. lit. judgment).

Hope overshadows our considerations even in the presentation of the images mentioned. As the seventh trumpet sounds loud voices in heaven proclaim: "The kingdom of this world has become the kingdom of our Lord and his Christ..." (Rev11:15). At this stage of the unfolding drama the victory over systemic evil is already certain and on its way.

CHAPTER FIVE

Anticipating the Kingdom

I saw a huge number of people of every nation, race, tribe and language dressed in white robes... standing in front of the Throne and the Lamb shouting salvation to our God and holding palms in their hands. 7:9

We may think that halfway through his vision John becomes very weary. It's demanding stuff. We have a hint of his likely weariness in the brief scene where he is asked to eat a little scroll (Rev10). It can well mean that in so doing he is sustained for the further receiving of the vision.

Furthermore, we can say that John is sustained and strengthened throughout the vision of the precipitating cosmic crisis by the incredible glimpses into heaven of the worship that is already taking place there. Likewise, we are sustained as he brings these glimpses to us in his letter and as we participate in the fullness of Christian worship on earth. The heavenly worship (in Rev4&5) surrounds the Throne of God and the Lamb. Again, the language is symbolic yet it is also real in its transcendent thrust. According to Revelation, we communally anticipate the coming Kingdom by worship. As we shall see, this is not an empty anticipation.

In Rev4 we see the twenty-four elders at worship; they represent the twelve tribes of Israel and the twelve apostles. So, the old and new covenants are indicated by the presence of the elders in the heavenly realm; their work is done and the covenantal action of God with humanity is completed. Then, the four living creatures appear, representing the animal world and the world of humans – they are singing day and night, "Holy, holy, holy is the Lord God who was, who is and is to come." (v. 8.)

In Rev7 there is the vision of the 144,000 of the tribes of Israel who have been sealed (vv.1-8). And, there is the huge number of people of every tribe and nation, who are dressed in white robes, surrounding the elders. "These are those who have come through the great tribulation… they shall never hunger or thirst again" (vv.9-17).

Are these visions of the present or of the future? The answer is that they are of both, for these things are happening now. That is, the in-gathering is beginning now and will be completed on the Great Day.

The purpose of the heavenly vision is to enable ENDURANCE: "you will experience tribulation, hunger and thirst – such as displacement and dispossession, but the life of community worship, in which you are in communion with the heavenly worship, will sustain you."

Hence there are windows[1] throughout the whole text to glimpse the activity of the heavenly realm, recurring in subsequent chapters (Rev14&19). In chapter 14 we are brought to Mount Zion and there standing on it is the Lamb with 144,000, singing a new hymn. Here they are the sum of the servants "who follow the Lamb wherever he goes" (v.4).

It is becoming clear that as the unfolding of the vision progresses the symbolism of numbers is important. Seven indicates completeness, as we have seen. The number, 144,000, is a complex of numbers, 12 x 12 x 1000. Twelve indicates perfection: God's purposes are achieved in the old and new covenants, represented by the two groups of elders around the throne. Then 1,000 represents an imprecise "many", a great number, ten being a general number, an approximation - hence 10 x 10 x 10 is a general number on a large scale.

"Enter the heavenly vision", John is saying to his readers. "Enter the company of praise", he is saying to the seven churches of Asia and to subsequent generations. "Behold, the redeeming action of the Lamb, the fullness of the triumph has already begun, fear not". More than this, "the faithful are already gathering in the courts above, can you hear their cries and shouts of joy… Heaven and her victory is so close to us on earth"!

---

[1] Some commentaries call these "interludes", a regrettable term that almost implies they are not necessary to the plot of Revelation.

Between the lines we can also imagine John saying, "the song of your victor, the *Kurios*, the Lord, is not that of the parading emperor, killing your brothers and sisters of the Faith. You fear the soldiers of that false victor who may stand at the door of your houses and knock, but, instead, be warmed and greatly encouraged by the true victor who stands at your door and knocks in order to enter in and sup with you. Do not be afraid."

In-gathering

John received his vision "in the Spirit on the Lord's Day" (1:10). Christians had already separated from the synagogues and had adopted the day of the resurrection for their day of worship, gathering to break the bread and share the wine. So, the new people of God were gathering for worship in the Spirit in order to join the celestial choirs and to be in chorus with them, sharing their victory song as they are given over to death in the present earthly realm. Hence in the congregations they knew that they were within the process of being gathered in.

The in-gathering that comprises all sorts of people, from the east, west, north and south – from every nation (7:9) – is a theme that is inaugurated in the prophets of the Hebrew scriptures and becomes a major focus in Jesus' ministry. The seeds of the theme of in-gathering in John's vision are planted in the book of Isaiah and the gospels.

The worshipful encounter on the Lord's Day does not remove the Christian pilgrim from the demands of speaking out about injustice; the Kingdom is offered to all and not a just a select few. The good news of the in-gathering must be expressed in the present in various forms, including standing up for the poor and oppressed. However, there are Christians in our times whose worship is labelled "in the Spirit" but detaches them from the demands of speaking out about injustice. These worshippers scarcely mention the harsh realities of the world and they orientate themselves to a narrow spirituality that tends to be expressed almost exclusively as "me and my Jesus - I am safe in his arms". In this way they remove themselves from the need to confront the social evils around them. This portrayal of worship pertaining to be "in the Spirit" is very different from that which John is describing. In the light of

John's vision this type of worship is not faithful but is sadly some cheap anomaly of the true way of worship that he portrays.

Feasting

The motif of in-gathering is imaged in terms of feasting.[2] This image in Revelation is presented as the marriage supper of the Lamb, in which the Bride, the faithful companion of the Lamb, is finally ushered in. In Isaiah 25:6-9, there is an amazing visionary prophecy of a future time of banqueting. John explicitly picks up this vison in Rev22.

When we turn to the gospels Jesus is seen feasting with people in a particular way. He begins his ministry eating and drinking with the outcasts and sinners of Israel ("table fellowship"). In this context he commences his proclamation and issues his invitation to the feast of God's Kingdom, pitched at this point in his ministry to the lowest and most rejected people in the society.

Eating and drinking with others was then, as it is now, a cultural sign of acceptance and hospitality. When Jesus feeds both 4,000 and 5,000 people in Mark and Matthew, a sign is presented of the in-gathering of not only the Jewish people but the Gentiles as well. The miraculous feedings display the divine generosity and welcome of salvation through him who is the Messiah. Here is Jesus' ministry of in-gathering.

In this discussion there is a rich set of connections that are held together in relation to Christian worship, the coming kingdom of God, the poor, and, eating and drinking. The key note at the heart of these collected themes is the concept of hospitality. Most cultures regard food and drink offered to friends, visitors and often strangers as a major sign of hospitality. It brings the host and those invited to share the food and drink into a close fellowship. On the basis of culture Jesus presents the world with **God's hospitality**. In this chapter it is important to trace how these themes are interconnected within the New Testament for they play a part in John's vision.

---

2 I am indebted to Geoffrey Wainwright, *Eucharist and Eschatology*, ch. 2, at this point.

Chapter Five - Anticipating the Kingdom

The gospel story builds on the hospitality offered by Jesus. The Last Supper stands in continuity with the table fellowship of Jesus with the people, but now the eating and drinking is focused upon his sacrifice: "this is my body, this is my blood". Jesus' sacrifice will from now on be the means of in-gathering: "when I am lifted up I will draw all people to myself" (John 12:32). His words and action with the disciples the night before he dies indicate that the consequent Lord's Supper of the early church will be the great sign of in-gathering.

Two teachings in the post-Easter period as recorded in the New Testament become relevant here: firstly, we see proof in the early church that the Lord's Supper is the central act of Christian worship that points to the in-gathering and secondly we find there is a special relationship established in the "eating and drinking" between the risen Lord and the believing community.

Let us look at each of these in turn.

Paul teaches, "Whenever you eat the bread and drink the cup you proclaim Christ's death until he comes (again)" (1 Corin 11:26). The Lord's Supper is a communal "looking-forward" to the End. After Pentecost the apostles and the early Christian community "share in the breaking of the bread" (Acts 2). Furthermore, the witness that Peter "ate and drank with him who had risen from the dead" (Acts 10:39) suggests that in the post-Easter period the Lord's Supper is readily understood as the central and regular practice of the Christian community in which they eat and drink with Christ (and in memory of him), anticipating the End-time of in-gathering.

Secondly, the Emmaus story (Luke 24) is significant in this regard. On the road the disciples had not recognised the risen Jesus. "While he was at table with them he took the bread, broke it and handed it to them. Their eyes were opened and they recognized him…" (vv.30-31). Christians are awakened to his presence in the celebrating of the Lord's Supper, "until he comes again". In other words, there is a special relationship bestowed on the believing, worshipping community with its risen Lord between his resurrection and the End, pointing to the One who welcomes outcasts and sinners, hence inviting them to participate now in the community as a foretaste to the final in-gathering to come.

John deepens this understanding by pointing to the heavenly worship which can be participated in now in the assembly on the Lord's Day. The presence of the risen Christ in worship is the same as the image in Rev1 of the Christ, "like a son of man", who stands among the lampstands, the seven churches of Asia. The presence and the power of the risen Christ in worship is identified with the expanded vision of the heavenly court and his victory as the sacrificed Lamb.

Manifestation of the Kingdom

The eucharist (literally, thanksgiving) therefore is a powerful sign of in-gathering. Worshipping in the Spirit we are intimately connected to the heavenly worship in which the beginning of in-gathering is already taking place and will be finalised in the future (the 144,000 that represents the vast throng). The eucharist is a pledge that this promise will be fulfilled in God's time.

The plot thickens in terms of meaning. More must be said. The Lord's Day, being Sunday, is understood as **the eighth day**, the new "day" inaugurated by Christ's resurrection - a powerfully anticipatory, tip-toe symbol. It is the day of the week within the new covenant in which we reach forward to the Consummation, centring on the "do this in memory of me." Be ready, therefore, as the warning is given: every Sunday since we are under judgment, do not dishonor the body of the Lord, present both in the eucharistic eating and drinking, and in the gathered community (1 Corin. 11:28-29).

When we come together on this "eighth day" in praise of God we are genuinely on the threshold of heaven, liminal-ly present to the New Creation that is fully to come. Sunday worship is not a prayer meeting wherein "most things go", as many Christians today like to think. Instead, it is an entry into the Kingdom, a manifestation of the Kingdom (Orthodox), in which the Church's fellowship with the poor and oppressed is held dear, echoing Jesus first table fellowship at the commencement of his ministry.

Chapter Five - Anticipating the Kingdom

The Orthodox Church has a lot to teach at this point. It is of interest that this great tradition of Eastern Christianity does not read from the book of Revelation in its services. "The Apocalypse is our life" – it provides the atmosphere and chief quality of Christian worship in its anticipatory dimension. Hence white robes, the altar, incense, chanting and the angelic hymns as well as prostration and bowing are incorporated into the eucharistic celebration. These elements are all included in John's vision. The Orthodox teach that the altar is placed in front of the people, not to be encircled by the people, since we are on pilgrimage to the Kingdom. The redeemed in Rev7:9 are "holding palms in their hands" - an indication that we are to use material things in worship, fresh from God's creation, like water, oil, bread, and wine, to express the truth of our redemption, that we are the first fruits of the new creation, of the harvest to come.

The Orthodox Church goes further in its close connection with apocalyptic thought exemplified in the architecture of churches (especially the dome), the icons and frescoes. In addition the Royal Doors, stationed between the congregation and the altar, open and close in the liturgy and are passed through, in and out by the priest, in order to express a dynamic association with the Kingdom: it can be entered now and it is to come.

Christ Pantocrator (1148 AD), mosaic, dome of Cathedral of Cefal, Palermo, Italy.

Within the dome the Pantocrator can be seen, a vast painting of Christ, the All-Ruler, which interprets "the thousand years" reign of Christ – see Rev 20:4. Painted in colour, the eyes of Christ are of particular significance. They are different from each other, one is of compassion and the other is of judgment. Standing beneath the fresco, worshippers know that they are in relationship with the Lord Christ who will judge them at the End but with mercy. The Apocalypse is our life!

Let us be reminded why worship, as being rich or full in the way described, is central to the life of faith according to John's vision. As Dorothy Lee puts it: "The fundamental spirituality of Revelation revolves around worship (which) entails sacrifice and obedience … Sacred ritual is not a delicacy to be enjoyed by aesthetes in the book of Revelation…True worship indicates where the heart lies: it becomes the foundation for radical action, behavior and lifestyle."[3] The worship is eucharistic and entails a manifestation, an anticipatory entry into the Kingdom.

---
3 Dorothy Lee, *Hallowed in Truth and Love*, p 227

Chapter Five - Anticipating the Kingdom

Refugee Christians can be seen to worship in this fullness of worship and they understand their faith accordingly. It has been extraordinary for me to have several years of accompanying the Karen people of Burma and to participate in their strong worship that seems to be, somewhat unconsciously to them, molded by the perspectives that are presented in Revelation.

I have been present at their Sunday worship both in refugee camps and in their resettled communities in Australia. Both circumstances indicate a freedom of the human spirit to be caught up into God and the heavenly places, but not in an escapist mode from the unjust realities of this world. The redeemed spirit that worships cannot be caged or imprisoned in refugee camps or elsewhere; it cries out (and plans) for freedom. To witness large numbers of Karen Anglicans on Sundays singing "Holy, holy, holy, Lord…" after the altar has been made ready with the gifts of bread and wine, and thanksgiving is sung by the priest - wondrously expresses the threshold of the Kingdom that is at hand in eucharistic worship, the mystical entering into the Kingdom through praise.

The fact that they are people with a refugee history is of course relevant here in the evolution of strong worship. This point is a reminder that we are all exiles to the Kingdom *and* on the path to the Kingdom, needing strong worship.

Finally, we can be reminded that in Revelation the coming Kingdom, although it is a great in-gathering of many, is essentially an intimate new world wherein there is a deep and loving union between Christ, his people and the created order. John expresses the union as **conjugal**.[4] With so many people gathered in it is hard to imagine what is being said here, but here it is! The mystical connection between Christ and his people, between the Lamb and his followers, is understood as a conjugal bond, namely, as the marriage supper of the Lamb. We are dealing

---

4 The marriage state is highly honoured in the Christian tradition mainly because it reflects the union between Christ and his people (Ephes 5:30f). Sexual union outside marriage, fornication, is seen, especially in Revelation, as a symbol of idolatry. Parts of the Hebrew scriptures indicate this sense, in particular, the prophetic parable of Hosea in which a man is married to a prostitute.

with an image of "conjugal" in relation to "consummation", as one is expressive of the other. The language is intentionally physical, we can even say, erotic. There is an arrived-at completeness of human life for all who are gathered in and for the whole of created life (consummation).

In the action of the eucharist the anticipation of the marriage supper of the Lamb is manifested, orientated to the End scene which is a luscious "spreading forth" of the New Creation in very physical imagery (Rev22). Alleluia! "Heaven and earth are full of your glory" ("the Sanctus" of the eucharistic liturgy).

Chapter Six

Accompanying the Martyrs

And the smoke of the incense, the prayers of the saints, rose before God. 8:4

What role do the saints and the martyrs play in the present time before the End? It becomes clear in the reading of the text that they are not simply a cheer squad of the Lamb who is now in heaven. What effect do their witness and deaths have?

The martyrs and the saints in Revelation appear at various points in the visionary narrative. The saints are identified as martyrs, so that the terms are coterminous. They share in Christ's sacrificial witness and in his victory. They are the followers of the Lamb. As we shall we see, they constitute "the core of the Church".[1]

To understand their witness and their role let us firstly leap forward to discuss two scenes that precede the Last Judgment and the Consummation (Rev21 & 22) and then go back to a scene in the opening of the seals (Rev6):

- - The Bride is prepared for the marriage supper of the Lamb
  - The Thousand Year Reign (Rev19&20)
- The saints pray under the altar (Rev6).

The Bride and the thousand year reign
Prior to the Consummation there is the scene of the defeat of the Dragon. In this scene we are told of the preparations of the Bride for the marriage supper of the Lamb in which the saints are closely associated with the Bride (19:7f).

---

1 Ellul, *Apocalypse.*

The Bride "has made herself ready" for the marriage supper to be the Lamb's bride (19:7). She is clothed in white linen which represents "the righteous deeds of the saints" (v.8).

In the Consummation scene that is about to take place there will be no distinction between the martyrs/saints and the rest of the people who have gathered. The former have fulfilled their role. The Bride is the Church at whose core reside the saints – they "have made her ready" and have brought her to this Great Day.

In the overall scene of Rev19-20 the forces of evil are finally overcome. The first resurrection takes place in which the reign of Christ covers a thousand years. The saints are described as those who have been beheaded for witnessing to Jesus, having preached God's Word and they now reign with Him (20:4). "The rest of the dead did not come to life until the thousand years were over" (20:5).

The "thousand years" in its symbolic meaning suggests a very long time (10x10x10). St Augustine in the fifth century interpreted this period as the time of the Church, its life and witness, between Pentecost and the End. This interpretation makes good sense. It is the first resurrection, and the second resurrection is the coming of the New Heaven and the New Earth.

Taking a literal understanding of the text here means that the forces of evil are not operative in the first resurrection period. At its conclusion the devil is let out from prison "to deal destruction." A symbolic understanding is required at this point - not to see the times and events as literally sequential but as inter-penetrative, with the time frames blending, presented in a vision-dream mode.

What is evoked in this passage is the sense that the saints are **reigning with Christ** in relation to the on-going sufferings in the world, in which they have participated sacrificially. Their "lives are hid with Christ in God" (Colos. 3:3). The first resurrection, the time of the Church, refers to the victory having being essentially won against the forces of darkness by Christ and yet bloody martyrdom continues until the End.

Chapter Six - Accompanying the Martyrs

The witness of the saints has the role of progressing the movement towards the End so that the Bride can be dressed and presented to the Lamb at the final marriage feast. A ripening is taking place - the imagery of the crop and harvest - as the saints are giving themselves in sacrificial prayer and witness prior to the End.

Under the altar

Earlier in John's vision the saints/martyrs appear when the fifth seal is broken (Rev6:10f): "I saw under the altar the souls of all the people who had been killed on account of the Word of God.[2] ... They shout with a loud voice, Holy Master and True, how much longer will you wait before you pass sentence and take vengeance for our death on the inhabitants of the earth?"

Each of them is given a white robe and is told to be patient for a little while longer until the roll is completed of their fellow servants who were still to be killed as they have been (v.11).

It is worth lingering on this passage. The souls of the saints, after their earthly lives, are pictured as "under the altar". The altar is the heavenly altar of the merit of Christ's sacrifice. They have witnessed to his saving death by their lives and their deaths, and now wait for the great and final Coming. They are not quite in heaven, it seems, or, they are in heaven in some particular sense. (Let us remember that there is the intermingling of earth and heaven as imaged in Revelation.) They are waiting for the Completion when others will be gathered into the New Heaven and New Earth. The saints are waiting, it may be preferable to say, in Paradise, the estate of the departed prior to the Consummation (see ch. 11).

"How much longer...?", they cry out; like the Psalmist, theirs is a notably human cry. They vividly remember the pain and injustice done to them on earth and their natural desire is to seek revenge, to have their heavenly Master administer revenge. They leave their request in

---

[2] The images of the saints 'reigning with Christ' and being 'under the altar' are not necessarily contrary to each other: the images are fluid in that they present different points about the departed saints.

the hands of God. Their anger may be momentary, directed towards "all the inhabitants of the earth" who have been complicit in some way in their deaths. The human touch here reminds the reader of their sacrifice and that saints are not dehumanized, spiritual souls but in fact have weaknesses like you and me. With this understanding of the passage it is suggestive of the notion that people like ourselves are called upon to witness even unto death.

The cry of the saints, "How long?" becomes a perennial cry of the servants of the Lamb as they come up against social and political evils. Referring to the witnessing Church through the centuries the words of the hymn, "The Church's One Foundation" ring true:

Though with scornful wonder
We see her sore oppressed…
Yet saints their watch are keeping
Their cry goes up, How long?
And soon the night of weeping
Will be the morn of song.

I have noticed over the years that Karen Christians sing this hymn in their own language and they really mean it. They sing it to the same melody as English-speaking people. The westerner, initially observing their worship may ask, "Why do they sing hymns that have come from Britain? Sure, the British brought the Gospel to Burma during the period of their rule, but why sing colonial hymns? Why not their own?"

Remaining a little longer in the worship, the westerner may well come to realise that the adopted hymns are truly baptized into their culture and spirituality. It becomes evident that, as an enculturated element of their worship, such adopted hymns are truly vehicles for them of devotion and praise amidst their own struggle to be faithful during decades of abuse and violence, and as they commemorate their own martyrs.

The perseverance of the saints in every generation summons subsequent disciples to endure, not just to put up with common suffering, but to endure in extending themselves in sacrificial prayer, witness and service.

Chapter Six - Accompanying the Martyrs

Furthermore, even **the prayers of the saints** (after death)[3], according to John, have meaning in terms of hastening the fulfilment of God's purposes, the flowering of the Kingdom into the fullness of consummated love. The departed saints pray "under the altar" for the coming of the Kingdom and hence for all who are stretching their lives in witness. The symbolism in Rev8:4-5 makes this clear.

John's main point here should be emphasized. We are asked to believe and know that the past witness of the martyrs/saints on earth, and now their prayers, are somehow, in the mystery of God's purpose, cumulative in terms of contributing towards the Coming of the Final Day. Hence the Bride, clothed with "the righteousness of the saints" is getting ready for the marriage supper of the Lamb, the time appointed by the Almighty for the in-gathering.

What does this topic mean for our contemporary lives? How do we better understand being a part of the Church that, for John, has the company and witness of the saints at its core? Clearly, John mentions these things in order that they may have an impact on the reader in every generation.

Modern-day saints/martyrs can help us develop a more vivid sense of the company of saints, their role and their prayers - for our own earthly journey.

On the west façade of Westminster Abbey the following twentieth century martyrs are presented in stone relief: Maximilian Kolbe, Manche Masemola, Janani Luwum, Grand Duchess Elizabeth of Russia, Martin Luther King, Óscar Romero, Dietrich Bonhoeffer, Esther John, Lucian Tapiedi, and Wang Zhiming.

---

3 Here there can be a moment of nervousness on the part of some protestants. The reformers were stringent in pointing out that Christ, as the sole mediator between heaven and earth, prevents any consideration of the effect or work of the saints, their witness and prayers (in life and in death) to progress the salvation of humankind. They were largely reacting to medieval excesses regarding the role of the saints. Also, they were not good exegetes of Revelation. It is time surely, after four hundred years since the Reformation, for a closer interpretation of the text of Revelation and to regard the saints as in Christ and not outside his mediatorial role.

The Apocalyptic Heart

Westminster Abbey - 20th Century Martyrs

Maximilian Kolbe is first of these modern martyrs depicted. In August 1941 Kolbe, a Polish Franciscan friar, volunteered to die in place of a stranger in Auschwitz Concentration Camp. He became the patron saint of drug addicts, political prisoners and prisoners.

Because of these martyrs' historical proximity to us in their witness to Jesus Christ we can be readily affected by what they stood for. They are fellow-travellers. They rest "under the altar" and a part of their prayer is "How long…?" They call us into a deeper communion with God and with them, and to a more courageous witness to hasten the ripening. Furthermore, the proximity of heaven and the coming Consummation is felt by being within the Communion of Saints. A traditional prayer of the Church expresses our relationship with them in these words:

May we be encouraged by their example,

strengthened by their fellowship

and aided by their prayers.

The Church's calendar provides a very helpful way to remember the saints/martyrs, and to incorporate the spirit of Christ that shone forth in their lives and deaths into our own journey.

Oppressed Christians profoundly remember their martyrs. It is interesting to note that St John Chrysostom, a great teacher in the Church of the fourth century, encouraged new Christians and inquirers to visit the tombs of the martyrs and there to receive healing (The Catechetical Orations).

Finally, we should ask ourselves, are the saints and the martyrs only a few? Do they amount to a clearly defined category? And what more can be said about what they are like?

The Orthodox (especially the Russian Orthodox) believe that what makes the Church distinctive is not its structure but holy lives. Along these lines Rowan Williams points out[4] that the saints are not an exclusive or select group but a vast, untidy workshop of sinners who are becoming holy – men and women who have often made grave mistakes but find the way to give themselves wholeheartedly in a singularity of direction to Christ's service. Saints are not typically balanced, well-rounded people (!), he writes, nor are they necessarily psychologically integrated. This is why we can be knocked off balance when we encounter a holy life. They are often despised in their own life-time and not just by "the empire" but by church authorities as well.

Sooner or later, Williams continues, we see in the saints a character of wakefulness to Christ's purpose and to the coming Kingdom which they have begun to enjoy. Sanctity and obedient discipleship in the Church is usually quite hidden. A deeper reflection, however, on "holy and faithful lives" helps us come to a clearer understanding of the Church as "the company of the holy and the faithful". By grace, God grants us a share in their company.

I believe that the thoughts here regarding the saints and the martyrs are basically consistent with Revelation's sense of who they are. Certainly, in John's time, in his understanding of them as servants of the Lamb within the Roman empire, their fate largely appears to be that of being beheaded. As martyrdom almost ceases at a later time, the saints, as those who live holy lives, are not put to death. In this historical sense then there is a difference between how saints and martyrs are understood in John's time compared to later. (A further discussion in relation to this point occurs in the next chapter.)

---

4 See Benjamin Myers, *Christ the Stranger, the theology of Rowan Williams*, ch. 8.

Let us be reminded that the purpose of the book of Revelation is largely to summon Christians to endure. By means of **the encouragement** of the witness of the saints/martyrs in every age, and their closeness to us within the mystical communion in Christ, we can endure: "Seeing we are surrounded by so great a cloud of witnesses, let us run the race that is set before us…" (Heb 12:1).

CHAPTER SEVEN

Silencing the Soul

And there was silence in heaven for half an hour. 8:1.

Interpretation, Martyrs and Monks

From the beginning of the third century Christian apocalyptic thinking was not emphasising fearsome and terrifying future happenings but rather it looked towards an awe-inspiring End-time.[1] The preaching of the early millenarian group, the Montanists[2], had waned. The predominant interpretation of apocalyptic thought in the following centuries was especially reflected in the icons and frescoes that appeared in the churches of the eastern regions of the empire.

Awe and hope were instilled in the minds of the worshippers. The Pantecrator (Christ the Ruler, "the all-embracing"), painted in the domes of churches from the fourth century, was a reminder to them of Christ in glory. The face of the Lord dominates as he looks down upon the worshippers and the world; his eyes are different – one displaying compassion and the other, judgment. Emerging from a period of varied interpretations of Revelation, the Church was developing a more positive approach to the book as a whole.

The major emphasis therefore by the end of the fifth century was on the redemptive work of Christ made available to all humanity and Christ's glory which is to be entered into now and fully in the future. In the Orthodox East, Revelation distinctively influenced these emphases and the place of the book was seen and used in different ways rather than as a text to be read in the services of worship. As "Word of God" it spoke

---

1 See Robert J Daly, *Apocalyptic Thought in Early Christianity.*
2 The Montanists were a second century movement that preached that the Heavenly Jerusalem would soon descend at a particular place. It is the first of other millenarian groups to follow.

into the Church's life through liturgical expression as well as through iconographical and architectural form.

In the West during later centuries the place of the book in the life of the Church was to take on different expressions, especially emphasizing punishment and hell as major emphases in John's vision. Parts of Revelation were included in bible lectionaries. Millenarian breakouts tended to be more prominent in the West than in the East of Europe.

The establishment of the Church in the empire in the fourth century (325) had a strong influence on the way in which apocalyptic thought was integrated in the life of the Church. We could say that the Church was tamed and that the outcry that is contained in the book against injustice and the forces of evil (of which empires are always complicit) became a voice that was less heard.

There was a dramatic decrease in Christian martyrdom. Devout Christians took to the deserts of Egypt, disturbed by the threat of the watering-down of the Faith, as crowds of people became baptised and filled the city churches. These desert disciples formed the beginnings of Christian monasticism which replaced martyrdom as the "second baptism" in terms of being the way to give your life sacrificially to Christ. Those who embraced the monastic way of life took vows of poverty, chastity and obedience (which became the established form of monastic identity). It entailed the giving of their lives through contemplation and prayer in the context of bonded community. The purpose was to find union with God, to taste the heavenly realm before death.

In the present era we are seeing the break-up of Christendom as the marriage of Church and State, and a return hopefully to the faithful witness of the Church that was seen in the first centuries. Christians are becoming more aware of the truths of Revelation, namely, of the clash between the victory of the Lamb and the forces of darkness, and the call to obedient discipleship. In the twentieth century there were more Christian martyrs that in any prior century.[3]

---

3 See Susan Bergman, *A Cloud of Witnesses.*

Apocalyptic silence

As we have seen in the opening of the seven seals (Rev6), John sees the vision of the four horsemen revealing the incessant cycle of war, famine and disease that causes massive destruction and havoc in every generation of humanity. Then, in a dramatic twist of mood and portent, he opens the seventh seal, and "there was silence in heaven for half an hour."

Within the numerology of John's letter "half" represents a short but significant length of time, a silence that falls after the strife and chaos depicted by the horsemen.

There is an icon of John receiving his apocalyptic vision that shows him covering his mouth in silence as though he is awe-struck at what he sees. What we see, with John, with the opening of the seventh seal amounts to a highly charged, poignant silence.

Why this silence, we may ask. What is its importance at this point in the visionary narrative? It is actually about the truth that God can do no more in showing the way of salvation in history than what God has done in the giving of the covenants.[4] Now, it is at last clear - it is the beginning of the Great End. The first covenant of the twelve tribes of Israel was followed by the second covenant of the twelve apostles (e.g.Rev4:10). We find ourselves within the second – it is the new covenant and it is the last. Christ has disempowered the powers of evil at their root and so the End is in view. The Holy Spirit is poured out to lead the way to the Consummation. What else can we do, given this realisation, but enter into the heavenly silence in utter awe for a short but a highly significant period of time.

The "half hour" is like a wedge planted between what has been and what is to come "soon", a wedge of awakened awe at the realisation of what has happened and now leads to the End; we are plunged into silence.

Silence then, in the Apocalypse of John, is in the face of and in response to God's action in history with the End in view. It therefore is a vital part

---

4 Hopko, *Apocalypse, The Book of Revelation in the Orthodox Tradition.*

of the Christian life, the life of contemplation and prayer. The ultimate victory must be countenanced and approached in a substantial moment of silence.

Silence becomes the deep route of the human heart in response to the revelation of God. St. Ignatius of Antioch in the second century taught, "Those who hear the Word of God through Jesus have to be silent." Now is the time for getting ready for the End and it must involve the discipline and joy of practicing contemplation that is both individual and communal.

Here we have a more fundamental reason for the practice of silence than that which was mainly taught in the fourth century and later, when monasticism began in the deserts of Egypt. The teaching then was important and cannot be discussed here. Nevertheless, in much teaching about silence over the centuries the apocalyptic emphasis that we receive from John has often been missing.

In contemplative silence we abandon our words, our thinking and our action in the face of God's determinative action. We enter the silence of heaven that takes place for a short, significant period. We are privy to the heavenly silence.

We can soon realise that it is a gift of intimacy. We read of this precious "half hour" in heaven so that we can enter into intimacy with the Lamb (Christ) and with the Father. We can find that an inner space develops within us wherein we can be detached for a time from the negativities that are always a part of our lives. We find that an awe and a bonded relationship with God grows, and this is both conscious and unconscious. It is not only a physical silence that we are thinking about here but an entering into the deep recesses of the heart to find the silence there.

This silence is not a luxury, only usable by those of the comfortable middle-class. It is a necessary part of the struggle and witness of being a Christian.

This chapter began with a glimpse into early church history and its apocalyptic thought. Within the monasteries of the eastern empire a kind of **interiorised apocalyptic** focus developed through a disciplined use of silence within the vowed life. According to this approach the events described in Revelation were viewed as a battle within the heart, mind and soul. The seven deadly sins[5] had to be engaged in a form of spiritual warfare. St Gregory of Nyssa, a fifth century monk and bishop, developed the notion of *epektasis:* stretching forward to the goal (of eternal life). This teaching gained its inspiration from St Paul's writing in Phil 3:12f: "I have not yet reached perfection, but I press on, hoping of that which Christ once took hold of me....forgetting what is behind me and stretching forward to what lies ahead." Gregory taught that the advancement made by the soul through spiritual struggle and growth (a moral, contemplative and mystical path) leads to the division between creature and Creator being overcome, attaining union with God.

I had an interesting encounter with a monk on the island of Patmos in 2014. A community of monks lives in the historic monastery that stands above the town and the Cave of Apocalypsis. As I was in the process of formulating this book I was determined to have a conversation with one of the monks about the book of Revelation and what it meant in their community life. Most of the monks there are Patmians so I assumed that the text of John's vision was of special importance to them. I found an English-speaking monk and asked him a question along these lines. His answer was to say that Revelation is a map that helps him find his way between good and evil; living as monks together, this map is given to us by St John who also taught us to base our lives on love (a reference to the Gospel and the letters).[6] It was a succinct answer, I thought, and sits in the monastic tradition that guides like Gregory of Nyssa and others have taught.

Silence and Action

Silence is not the opposite of action. Action must be always refilled with love and silence is the key to this refilling.

---

5 The deadly sins are: pride, covetousness, lust, envy, gluttony, anger, sloth.
6 See the brief discussion in ch. 1 about the Johannine circle.

Thomas Merton, the twentieth century American monk and writer, one day left his monastery where he had practiced silence for many years. He made a visit to the local town. As he walked in the main street he was suddenly overwhelmed with love for those who passed him by. Later he described it as a remarkably memorable sense of love which expanded within him towards all humanity; for him it was a kind of epiphany. A good definition of "epiphany" is the flooding in of light into a situation, the flooding of light of the coming New Heaven and New Earth.

We are called to let mystical experience arise in us from the practice of silence in order to fuel our journey of action and witness. Silence is required to help us enter the compassion of God for aching humanity, as Merton discovered as he walked in the street of the local town. We are not refilled usually by urgent asking or trying to make spiritual experience happen, but rather by emptying ourselves to receive God's grace in and through silence.

The grace of silence is End-orientated, bringing assurance that all is in God's hands. We can access the peace, the rest that God has in store as we seek to be actively faithful.

Silence is needed for non-violent action, the way of the Lamb. To act non-violently in peace-making we must be contemplative. Silence, by means of its gentle work prepares in us what St Paul calls "God's armour" (Ephes. 6:11-17): "the sword of faith, the breastplate of righteousness and shoes to proclaim the gospel of peace."

Michael Ramsay, one-time Archbishop of Canterbury, once said that in his hourly meditation every morning it was only in the last five minutes that he sensed the peace of God. The five minute period is "gold" in which he and other meditators are in touch again with the non-violent path of forgiving enemies and peace-making.

As we think about silence and action being hand in hand, I cannot but help contrast, "There was silence in heaven for half an hour" with two other verses in Rev 12:7, "And war broke out in heaven", and v.10, "I heard a loud voice in heaven…"

Chapter Seven - Silencing the Soul

Rev12 is like a half-way point within the whole cosmic drama of Revelation. The "sevens" of the seals, trumpets and bowls have taken place. The final battle against the beasts and the Whore of Babylon, is about to begin. The chief beast, the Dragon, appears with seven heads and seven horns, and comes before the heavenly woman who has given birth to a male child. The child is snatched from her and is taken to God while the woman flees into the wilderness to a place prepared by God.

"War breaks out in heaven" – Michael and his angels fight the Dragon, throwing him and his angels down upon the earth. A loud voice proclaims in heaven, "Salvation has come, the accuser is thrown down and is conquered by the Lamb and his followers" (12:11).

The momentary silence in heaven (that we have been discussing) commemorates what God has done in history. It can also be seen as anticipating what lies ahead in terms of the final action of God - enabling the End to unfold.

Strangely, in the scene of Rev12, we see the Dragon in heaven (v.7). We may need reminding at this point that the tradition speaks of the devil being a fallen angel. At the Creation God allows the angels and human beings to take responsibility for the wellbeing of the world. The Domination System emerges in which fallen spirits take power and humankind capitulates with this rule. But now at last is the moment of God's final action and the collapsing of the System.

Let us return to the plight of the heavenly woman. Suddenly, we see her clothed with the sun, the moon beneath her feet and on her head are twelve stars. She is the female figure who accompanies the saving work of her son and is included in the triumph.

She has been likened to faithful Israel, to Mary and to the faithful Church. She bears her child who will rule. In whatever way this woman is identified there need not be one absolutely right interpretation. Again, John's imagery here is polyvalent. The image is feminine. In our time faithful, quiet and bold service can be pictured as "this woman". The role of Mary as Madre de los Desaparecidos (Mother of the Disappeared) in El Salvador and Our Lady of Guadalupo in Mexico, are appropriate associations with her. She holds and supports the unjustly treated in her prayers. In the centuries leading up to the incarnation of Christ, when Israel was in continual strife, there were the faithful *anawim* of the Lord - the remnant faithful who were poor and yet served in prayer and loving witness to their faithful God. These too are the heavenly woman.

The action of God is accompanied by those who serve in humble ways and by their silent prayer, at the heart of which sits the "half hour of silence" in heaven.

Chapter Eight

Witnessing the Structures Fall

The merchants who had made a fortune out of Babylon stood at a distance... mourning and weeping. 18:15

"Witnessing the Structures Fall" is the carefully chosen title for this chapter. We are dealing here with the sweep of chapters 13-20 in John's vision. The three beasts – the dragon, the beast from the sea and the false prophet - appear on the cosmic stage to rage and wreak havoc in response to the Lamb and his followers. Babylon[1], the Earthly City, and its whore are presented. All the corrupt ways of Babylon are displayed. The structures that have been developed and maintained by these forces, symbolically presented, must eventually fall according to God's plan.

It is not easy for some people to read or listen in these chapters to the raging clash between the forces of evil, represented in these images, and the forces of God. I indicated in the early chapters of this book that for the Karen refugee youth with whom I was leading a study on Revelation, an assurance was needed to "see the story through" to the good end: we had the refrain for each session, "isn't it wonderful that the Lamb defeated the Beast".

For John's original hearers in the seven churches of Asia he had chosen violent imagery to depict the divine victory; imagery that would convey that there is a power even stronger than the might of Rome. The youth know trauma first or second hand. Although they did not want to be exposed to violence again they nevertheless wanted to see God as victor in their situation of oppression. The imagery in John's vision can

---

[1] Babylon was where the Jewish people were captive in the exile of the sixth cent. B.C. It, as the haughty empire, would be "destroyed" (Jer 25:12f). It then becomes a metaphor of the corrupt city or empire, historically identified as Rome in John's vision but also is generic of satanic deception and power in other and various empires.

connect constructively to refugee people in their ambivalence about being exposed to violence. The following story will help to explain.

At a weekend camp in Australia for Karen (resettled) refugee women a bishop had visited to guide the group in learning about meditational prayer. After an initial practice a woman explained that when she closed her eyes her mind became dominated by images of Burmese soldiers attacking her home village. Even after six years in her resettled, safe country she still suffered from these traumatic memories. She had this day-dream regularly and we can suspect she had it as a night-dream at times as well.

John's dream-like medium of presentation comes alongside the experience of oppressed people and any who suffer from forms of trauma; it speaks into their present condition powerfully and with promise.

Continually, we must see that the imagery is symbolic to a significant degree. That unjust structures must fall is clear in John's vision and can be taken literally. The descriptions of how they will fall, however, must be taken symbolically. There are some clues, as we shall see, that John intends us to understand his plot in this way.

We have seen that the Domination System of the principalities and powers is the basis of the conflict. By means of the work of Jesus Christ the purpose of God is set in motion to achieve the victory of God, to restore the wholeness of creation. Jesus broke "the bars of iron" that have held humans in bondage; the rolling, destructive repetitions of history in terms of war, famine, disease and death are confronted such that their days are numbered. Humanity has colluded with the powers in establishing patterns of destructiveness in every generation. But a new humanity is born of Christ's resurrection and he calls this new "breed" into renewed obedience and courage as he stands among the lampstands (the churches) and summons.

Hence the book of Revelation is a vital component in the canon of the New Testament. In its symbolic language the dimensions of the struggle between the forces of evil and God are exposed in ways that are indicated but not fully presented in other parts of the New Testament. This fuller display, by means of vision, is particularly to do with encouraging believers to be strong now so that the strangle-hold of the powers upon the world, having been broken, may be finally overcome.

In this regard Rev13-20 presents us with what looks like another form of **intensification**.[2] The images of the three beasts, the trinity of evil, and the exalted collaboration of the Earthly City with them present a form of warfare that is directed against the servants of the Lamb. Here is a form of intensification that builds on what has come before. It is in the face of the attacks of the beasts and Babylon that the servants of the Lamb persist, are beheaded *and* at the same time join in the heavenly choirs that in heaven gather around the immolated, triumphant Lamb.

Let us again be reminded that the categories of "heaven" and "earth" are not distant from each other in Revelation. As a consequence of the event of Christ they are brought into a form of dramatic interaction. This changed cosmic structure is orientated forward into the emerging of universal harmony by the will of God and the work of the Lamb.

The images of the beasts are despotic images. The dominating powers will fight to the death because they have enjoyed their privileges for millennia. They therefore will mock the Lamb and his followers – the seven headed dragon has one head which resembles that of the Lamb, intended to elicit in the people: "follow me, I will bring you pleasure and security, I can give you more instant satisfaction than you can have by accompanying the Lamb."

The lure presented in the vision at this point goes further. The whore of Babylon does not just appear as an every-day-type prostitute. She is the Great Prostitute who exults and parades the luxuries of the City's wealth. She represents a diabolical parody of love - it is a false love that is bound up with the power of money and its corrupt usage. She is the

---

[2] We have seen intensification in the progression of the seals, trumpets and bowls – now it occurs with the symbolic forces described in this chapter with the focus of evil being finally overcome by the Lamb and his servants.

opposite of the woman and her child – Rev12[3] - who are symbols of the love of God. The whore is the seducer - she holds a cup and in doing so claims to establish communion, to attract the people into the false communion that she and the Great City offer.

The sin of greed is manifested so strongly in the scene. Already the reader may be thinking of how this can refer to aspects of modern culture with the flaunting of excessive greed in western society and beyond.

At the time of John's vision, Rome was the focus of the vision of the Earthly City, as it is received by late first century believers. "Babylon" is also "the city" in every generation wherein some people acquire enormous power and wealth at the expense of others and they collude to maintain the structures that suit them and do so to the point of using violence. A false culture grows. It is therefore up to us to discern in our generation where the abuse of power like this lies.

But now has come the time to mourn. The City is falling – in God's time, according to the accumulating witness of the followers of the Lamb. The merchants weep as they see the City being destroyed before their eyes, as their accrued wealth and possessions crumble, disappearing to be buried beneath the earth. They are bystanders, beholding the event before them. The seafarers and artists similarly mourn as bystanders viewing all that is being lost in the collapse of the City. They have had their advantages and privileges as they complied and benefited within the corrupt state, at cost to others.

Let us particularly notice that these groups who have enjoyed the City's wealth are bystanders, "they stand at a distance" (Rev18:5). They are not destroyed along with the City. The structures fall and are destroyed but they as humans, although they have been complicit in the corrupt ways of the city, held in the grip of the powers, are not destroyed. They are preserved.

God is the hidden actor or performer in Revelation. It is the angels that are pictured sending forth heaven's final resistance to the negative forces

---

3 See the discussion on the woman and child in the previous chapter.

Chapter Eight - Witnessing the Structures Fall

arrayed in the world. God is not the direct agent in John's vision but at the same time it is God's decision to deal finally with the powers once and for all.

The violence to humans is a concern to many readers of John's letter. We can note that already the humans who benefit from the corruption of the city are spared and will progress to the divine judgment. There is still time for them to repent and come to God. Very graphic images in this section of the letter, however, need explanation where there are scenes that depict heaven's administering of violence to humans.

A significant example is found when we arrive at 19:11f. We are presented with a visionary scene that culminates in "all humanity being destroyed." It is a part of the last battle. It is in fact imagery that is intended to portray the persistence of the purposes of God to deliver victory and redeem. It is good to ask in this context, "how the persistence of God's purpose functions in the face of what seems like impossible odds?" We see the grotesqueness, the massive power of the empire, its habits of violence. But God's ways, it is now claimed, are as great – no, they are greater. God's might in and through the Lamb and his followers, although it is less visible and seemingly weak, is actually stronger. Graphic apocalyptic imagery is used to convey complete persistence.

The scene begins with the appearance of the white horseman. As it is traditionally interpreted[4] this image is that of Christ. He is described as having his cloak soaked in blood (v.13). In other words, it is Jesus Christ, the Son of God, who has had the destructive forces taken upon himself on the cross, suffering the deadly consequences of violence. He is the one who dies for all. (Rom 6:10). There is a purpose to this subjection: by his wholly just and loving life and death he has broken "the bars of iron" that have imprisoned humankind in its cyclical character.

The symbolically dramatic nature of the scene is most clearly expressed in the appearance of "the sharp sword" that comes "out of his mouth" (v.15). Why, out of his mouth? It is the same sword as the one coming

---

4 Interpretation at this point has been prominently given by the church fathers of the 4-5th centuries.

out of the mouth of the apocalyptic Christ in Rev1, as he stands among the lampstands (the seven churches). This sharp sword is the Word of God that "cuts through ... to sift the purposes of the heart" (Hebr 4:12). It is what enables disciples in every generation to stand before despots and name the truth of "empire" and the lasting truth of God's Kingdom, as Jesus did standing before Pilate. Or to work with compassion and justice among suffering people. It is the Word of God that inspires and upholds. Christ continues to wield it until the End. This is the meaning of "him treading the fury of the wrath of Almighty God" (v .15).

Let us look briefly at a few examples of how Christians have stood up and addressed the tides of injustice, and in particular, the greed and structures of greed in their time.

In the early thirteenth century St Francis and St Dominic emerged as preachers at a time when the Church in Europe was largely rural. But it was a time also when the Church was faced with growing numbers of people gravitating to the cities, attracted to work prospects due to new means of production (similar to the Industrial Revolution in the nineteenth century). New patterns of wealth and poverty developed. Francis became a travelling preacher, proclaiming the freeing gift of poverty and the simplicity of the love of God. Dominic preached a purified faith, a distilled truth with which the people could find their spiritual path amidst the changes and confusion that they found in a different society.

In the early twentieth century the young, emerging Swiss theologian, Karl Barth, criticised the rising capitalism of Europe and the misuse of the advancing technology, which he named "a playful arrogance". Specifically, he applied this term to the construction of the *Titanic* with its swimming pools and shopping malls. Its sinking was "the judgment of God", he preached at the time in his parish church in Switzerland. Humans inflict the tragedy on themselves through their pursuit of greed: this is the judgment of God.

Barth called for a form of communal labour as a sign of Christ's Kingdom, in order to curb the growing number of large companies and the corrupt exploitation of factory workers that he saw taking place in his own town.

In a similar fashion Pope Francis, in 2013 (and more recently) has called for the transformation of international capitalism due to it being the major form of structural greed in the world of the early twenty-first century.[5]

Rev13-20 develops the flavor of the last battle, the battle, according to John, that we find ourselves in now. He uses traditional apocalyptic language. We may ask, is there a presentation of Armageddon in Revelation? Rev19 comes closest to it. Yet here it is not in the classical, Jewish form of a cosmic violent battle but the scene is altered into a Christian trajectory. The mythological image of "all humanity is destroyed" is being re-interpreted as symbolic of the absolute divine determination to see justice on earth The whole scene at this point is characterised by the symbols being used differently, namely, of a victory to be interpreted with a non-violent meaning: the Christ proclaimed and enabled way of peace and justice.

The period of time is the Last Days, from Pentecost until the End. We find ourselves in the period between the times of Christ's first coming and his second coming. There is a kind of apocalyptic intensification of the clash between the forces of evil and of God within the history. We need to say "a kind of" since it is not the intention of Scripture that we correlate the intensification in Revelation with what may appear in our opinion as examples of "intensification" in the course of history, such as in the present time.

We have before us a paradoxical matter in this regard. In this century we are facing certain global challenges for the first time in world history, challenges that appear to be "apocalyptic" - in other words, they are threatening the life of the planet (in this sense in which the word is often

---

5 Pope Francis is blunt, naming "a (global) economy of exclusion and inequality... such an economy kills; a culture of prosperity deadens us... As long as the problems of the poor are not radically resolved by rejecting the autonomy of markets and financial speculation... no solution will be found for the world's problems." Cited in *Sojourners*, August 2014.

used). There are the vast, increasing numbers of refugees as millions flee violence in their homelands. Then there is the growing devastation due to climate change. What is the future, given these world-wide trends? They can cause people to wonder whether it is God's plan is to culminate the planet's history sooner rather than later.

Again, however, we must say that we "do not know the day or the hour… not even the Son knows the day or the hour" (Mark 13:32).

Revelation holds out to us a more major consideration than that of attempting prediction. It emphasises the call to faithful discipleship, including seeking to address these big issues - to go forward in the light of God's faithfulness to see his Creation find its fulfillment, and with us being a part of this holy purpose.

Chapter Nine

Responding to the Books Opened

The Book of Life was opened. The dead were judged according to their works as recorded in the books. 20:12

A commentator has written of John that he was in danger of knowing too much, having toured heaven! The last paragraph of Rev20 is the climax of his vision. The devil is at last thrown into destruction and the dead, great and small, are raised to stand before the Throne of God. The Book of Life and the books are opened and all are judged according to their deeds (v12).

These are astounding pictures imaging the final overthrow of evil's domination and of summoning readers to respond to the finality of God's victory by seeing themselves – ourselves – judged before the Throne of God. John, it appears, maintains his sanity in his tour of heaven.

Death and Hades, the temporary abode of the dead, are destroyed (v14); the Consummation then unfolds before our eyes.

Central to the reading of these events is the call to readers in every generation prior to the End to know they must give an account of how they lived their lives, believers and non-believers alike.

The enormity of the images continue, precipitated by the final conquest of God over all evil forces – The New Jerusalem shall come down from heaven, that which has endured as honorable in the nations will be brought into the heavenly city which is now on earth: "the glory and honour of the nations will be brought into it" (21:26). The peace and justice that God has so yearned for to be established in this world, flares into being; the Kingdom of God fully arrives.

Some years ago I heard a woman on the radio being interviewed. She was being asked about her role as an aid worker in East Timor. She described how her present work had changed her life and that there was no looking back to desire a more comfortable existence. At one point the interviewer asked: "What motivates you to do your work?" The woman replied, "When I come to stand before my Maker at the Last Judgment what could I say about being faced with this opportunity in my life and I did not take it." It was a brave reply within the context of the highly secularised culture of western media.

The story reminds us that to read about the books being opened with our deeds already recorded, evokes challenges for us in the present, challenges requiring serious consideration to take risks and step out of our comfort zones in forms of service that the Spirit lays before us. Furthermore, to dare to proceed down the path offered, can have the potential to turn around our lives as the woman being interviewed described was the case for her. The "turning around" is towards work that announces the love, peace and justice of the coming Kingdom.

The mystery of God's final judgment that is pointed to in the images of Rev20 is a subject that can occupy the minds of the Christian refugee people with whom I work. They sometimes, ask, "will the non-believers be saved?" The question largely arises from their background as Karen church people living in Burma, belonging to a minority religion and persecuted in a predominantly Buddhist society. They have been at times exposed to the defiant attitude of some Christian preachers who presented an excessively narrow view of personal salvation.

Referring to the often repeated case of people, say, in remote jungle parts of their own country, who have never heard the proclamation of Christ, I once asked a Karen audience, "Will God finally reject them?" The Rev20 text indicates that God will look at the record of their deeds in order to judge them. Fr Tom Hopko makes the remark colourfully in his series on apocalyptic thought[1] that many may have heard a version of the Good News but it is scarcely a true and wholesome version, hence they have had no opportunity to respond. God will judge according to people's deeds. This judgment is God's business, not ours.

---

1 *The Book of Revelation in the Orthodox Tradition.*

Chapter Nine - Responding to the Books Opened

We are not faced here with a lessening of the urgency of sharing the Good News in evangelistic work. God desires all to come into the gracious fellowship of Jesus Christ now, to pray and work for the hastening of the Coming of the Kingdom.

Protestant teaching emphasises that we are justified by faith – set right with God by our response of faith to the free offer of grace, and that we are not set right with God by our works. St Paul's letter to the Romans goes to lengths to propound this notion. The image of the Book of Life being opened to issue judgment according to our deeds has to be balanced with Paul's doctrine, within the scope of New Testament teaching. A solution to the tension here is given by St James. The letter of James provides the reminder that faith without works is dead faith – faith requires a life of good deeds.

In all of this kind of discussion there lies at the core of the scriptures the sense that God looks on the human heart in order to draw all people to himself and renew the whole creation.

A question that comes to mind usually about ourselves and final judgment is to do with time: "What happens to me when I die and the Last Judgment awaits me in the future?" Karen Christians helpfully have maintained the language of "sleeping (or resting) in Jesus" (1 Thessal 4:14). This phrase has been in use in church circles in the West but seemed to have disappeared some decades ago. In our living, our dying and our deaths, we await the Last Judgment and Consummation. Waiting in death for the final things is such that we go to God "in the crowd" and not as individuals but together with the martyrs who as we saw in ch 6, longingly await the Consummation (Rev 6).

We are touching here on the notion of "the intermediate state", also named "paradise", the Gate of heaven, wherein earthly time no longer exists since the dead are in eternity (see 2 Pet 3:8). The New Testament presents us with a rich fabric of our pre-End existence, whether in this life on earth or departed: we already taste the heavenly gift (Hebr 12:12, Rev7, 14:5...) and are already in Christ (John14:2f, 2 Corin 5:8, Phil 1:23).[2]

"Hades", the temporary abode of the dead, and Death are "thrown into the lake of fire" (Rev.20:14) We read in the first letter of Peter that Christ goes to preach to the spirits in Hades, the underworld, thus bringing them to the final judgment (3:19, 4:6).

We are here taken back to John's initial vision – of the risen Christ (1:18) who is given the keys of Death and Hades. Hades was "the place" of shadowy, hopeless waiting; now the intermediate state, Paradise, is "the place" of hopeful, expectant waiting.

The notion of purgatory as a dimension of the intermediate state claims to have its foundation in the scriptures, especially in 1 Corinth 3:10-15: "the Day of the Lord will be revealed with fire, and the fire will test the sort of work each has done." Joseph Ratzinger in his book, *Eschatology, Death and Eternal Life*,[3] moves away from the old medieval notion of purgatory as "a place" and provides a helpful consideration of this passage: in death we are the recipients of the divine mercy; "the fire" is the encounter with the Lord - this is transformation (there is no other "fire"); it is the fire that burns away our dross and reforms us to be vessels of eternal joy (p. 231). A part of a discussion here is to regard our prayers on earth for the departed as a natural consequence of them being in the intermediate state and of our ongoing concern for them.

In the midst of our picturing judgment and in the mist of our striving to be servants of the Lamb, we are encouraged to turn ever more deeply to the risen One and "to fall at his feet", as he says, "do not be afraid ...

---

2 Paradise has had various meanings attached to it over the centuries: the Garden of Eden, the New Heaven and New Earth, heaven and the intermediate state. A part of the reason for this fluidity of meaning is the uncertainty of interpretation of Jesus' words to the rebel at the crucifixion, "this day you will be with me in Paradise" (Luke 23:43). Many find it helpful to have the word used to refer to the intermediate state.
3 Catholic University of America Press, 1988.

Chapter Nine - Responding to the Books Opened

I am the first and the last." (1:17,18). The Spirit is the down payment[4] since the resurrection of Jesus, the guarantor of the things to come, our advocate along the way.

More needs to be said to make sense of the Christian understanding of judgment.

John's vision of the Last Judgment presents itself as fulfilment of the limited picture of "the Day of the Lord" in the Hebrew Scriptures. There, in the prophetic writings, the Day of the Lord involves judgment and punishment of the enemies of Israel (e.g. Isa 11:10, 19:19-25, Micah 3:3.) In John's vision, however, there appears before us the great division, in this, the second and final covenant - the last dispensation of God in the world. It will be to cut though Israel, the nations AND the churches. All will be judged in the merciful sifting of the people of the earth, in righteousness wherein God's justice is tempered by love.

A word on hell. The concept as an eternal punishment state has a degree of backing in some New Testament passages. Jesus also used the image of Gehema for hell, which was a rubbish tip outside Jerusalem. God's final judgment tragically implies that "some will not make it" to the final redemption. The creation of the human being at the beginning with free will is maintained; God's providence maintains the dignity of the human being as a free agent even when in the course of history human freedom is threatened by the Domination System of greed and violence. A harsh notion like "absolute god-forsakenness retains a place in the renewed creation"[5] has to be recognised, being in accordance with the existence of human free will. These matters are difficult to speak about. Our liberal thinking, western culture finds such concepts difficult to accept, but face them we must.

We are touching into the mystery which we scarcely dare enter. After all, final judgment is God's business not ours. The apostles agreed with this since we find no mention of hell in the Acts of the Apostles. The task is to grasp redemption and its path in the present.

---

4 Berkoff, *The Christian Faith*.
5 Ellul, *Apocalypse*.

The post-world war two theologian Karl Barth was emphatic about the extent of Christ's work on the cross to save humanity. He wrote of the crucifixion of Jesus as the limitless mercy of God on the human creation, limitless in reaching even into the dark depths of the human heart to rescue and redeem; the arms of the Saviour are wide –stretched indeed.

Therefore, the considerations that I have drawn attention to here need to be kept in a careful balance; our task after all is to follow and to leave these mysteries to the wisdom and mercy of God.

I have entitled this book, *The Apocalyptic Heart,* which seems appropriate especially at this point, as we ponder these things. God seeks and seeks again to redeem all of the creation, as much as it is at all possible, as history continues to go forward and will come to its end. We are invited urgently to take these things to heart (Rev1:3).

The key-note that we are left with in these musings as we see the books opened and share the poignant rumour with others – is to feel the call to faithful, courageous servanthood of the Lamb and to respond without delay.

Chapter Ten

Delighting in the Consummation

I saw a new heaven and a new earth. 22:1

The curtain opens on the new order breaking through in this world (Rev 21). The marriage feast of the Lamb has begun. Now we are presented with the more expansive image with the appearance of the New Heaven and New Earth – "the old has passed away" – and the New Jerusalem is coming down from heaven, "prepared as a bride adorned for her husband."

Why "Jerusalem"? Why is the great Consummation named by this city, and as "new"?

Jerusalem (literally, City of Peace) continues to be, even in the twenty-first century, the place where there exists an extraordinary intense meeting-point between worship and political conflict. The worship is maintained by three world religions, Judaism (especially), Christianity and Islam. Over centuries with the temple at its centre many have written about the city.[1]

That her conflict would end was the prayer of Jesus at the Mount of Olives as he looked over the city and entered it to go to his death.[2] She is the heart-beat of the human mix that worships God and at the same time is drawn into violence. She represents this humanly unsolvable mix. Her time came for resolution with Christ's sacrificial death and now the peace of Jerusalem (and of the whole world) is to come down as a gift from heaven. Her warfare is over.

---

1 See Nizar Qabbani, cited in Simon Sebag Montefiore, *Jerusalem*, especially p. 602.
2 "Jerusalem, Jerusalem, you who kill the prophets and stone those sent to you, how often I have longed to gather your children together, as a hen gathers her chicks under her wings, and you were not willing." Luke 13:34.

The invitation is given, "Come, all you who are thirsty" (v.6),"Come all who have conquered" (v.7). Excessive evil-doers have been severely judged at the Last Judgment. But the faithful who have endured in the seven churches and in the churches in subsequent generations are welcomed. "The thirsty" are invited and they represent those who have been poor and did not have clean water to drink, who thirst for justice (Matt 5:6); these are the downtrodden who had no chance in earthly life due to human neglect and cruelty within the Domination System – they are now welcomed to the Kingdom of Justice.

"Thirsty" is an image that brings together different conditions of poverty. It represents not only a lack of water but "needy when there is water" - conditions like an over-abundance of dangerous water (viz. refugee boat people) and dirty water that creates thirst because to drink it creates deadly disease. As Richard describes from his Latin American experience; "… the poor die in floods because they are pushed out of safe places and forced to live alongside rivers, plagues such as cholera and tuberculosis fall primarily on the poor who … lack sanitation infrastructure".[3] "Come, all you who are thirsty."

Hope arises from what we and the poor read at this end portion of John's vision. "The angel showed me the river of the water of life, as clear as crystal…" (22:1). As well as being a spiritual image of God's grace flowing, "the river of the water of life" can bring hope for the poor to look forward to clean, flowing water, hopefully not only in the future Kingdom but in this life. Then, we see the walls of the city have foundations based upon the twelve apostles and the city is square (v.16) to represent the equality of all the redeemed people of God (Rev22).

The invitation "to come" is intimated earlier in John's whole vision:

"And I looked and a great multitude that no one can count, from every nation, tribe, people and language are standing before the Lamb" (7:9). Matthew's Gospel has a similar vision. A major overall theme there

---

[3] Pablo Richard, *Apocalypse*, p. 86

Chapter Ten - Delighting in the Consummation

consists of the gathering-in of the nations.[4] Abundant numbers from every nation, large and small, will be gathered in.

This multicultural vision has implications for the present: seeing the vison leads to being inspired for action in the present. The prophet John, Matthew and others in the New Testament provide the call to present-day churches to reach across ethnic barriers to embrace those of other cultures as brothers and sisters who belong to the coming New Jerusalem, including refugees. Multicultural encounter and unity in the present is a powerful anticipation of that which is to come, and, some argue, hastens the Day of the Coming. This challenge cannot be taken up in a cursory or superficial way. Rather, it is to be done by reaching out patiently and with "ears wide open", to listen to the struggles, the stories that the newcomers yearn to share. In this encounter there are rewards for all parties.

Our natural questioning may again ask at this point - when will the Day arrive? In ch. 2 we explored the notion of "soonness" and the need in every generation to maintain hopeful expectation. John's whole vision suggests that it will be the increase of saints and martyrs that will constitute the readiness of the Bride and until that time there will be "a delay". The saints and the martyrs cry out "How long" (Rev6), yet it is their witness that through successive generations accumulates in history and will lead to the divine decision to culminate history – to endow it with the gift from above in the form of the New Jerusalem.

However, there is continuity and discontinuity at this mysterious future point on the plane of history. Much that has been of value in the nations will be included in "the New". At the same time the first fruits of "the New", who are the wide company of saints and martyrs, are now vindicated. The poor, or "thirsty", together with all globally who have passed through judgment, are ushered in. The God who comes in history at the incarnation of Christ comes at the end of history to

---

4 In his gospel the theme gets underway with the Visit of the Wise Men (ch2) which represents and foreshadows the gathering-in; then towards the end of the gospel in ch.25 there are the three parables of the Coming Kingdom of God – "Before him shall be gathered all the nations…" and 28:19 is also to be noted.

restore all things in Christ. The risen Christ who stands in heaven and on earth amongst the churches is now the married Lamb. Mystically he is equated with "the fullness of God" in a renewed earth, imaged in the pictures of the renewal that John paints here in chs 21 & 22. Christ fills all things and the Spirit says "Come".

The image of light is highly significant in the picture that is contained in these two final chapters of Revelation. God's light shines; there is no need for the sun by day (22:5). With increased numbers of witnesses the time will come, with the judgment, when the light of God will flood and fill all things.

The very final picture in John's letter begins with these words: "the Spirit and the Bride say, Come". An extraordinarily graceful invitation is issued: "whoever wishes, let them take the free gift of the water of life" (22:17). The gates of the New Jerusalem are not yet closed, still awaiting further pilgrims, whoever they are.

The many, being ushered in, are understood in Eastern Orthodoxy in terms of a rich theological tradition, namely of "becoming divinized".[5] Divinisation can occur in the Christian life prior to the Consummation, as the soul progresses, bathed in the light of God, being purified and enlightened, beginning in baptism. Saints, such as St Seraphim of Sarow (19th cent.), became flooded in light, arriving at a point of outwardly glowing with light, illumined by the light within, as witnessed by the disciples who followed him.[6] Furthermore, the condition of holiness to which we are called is envisioned by St Gregory of Nyssa after death as a state of rest-in-motion. In this state we shall still be growing, according to Gregory, and at the same time be filled with grace. This notion of a "motion-ful rest" is consistent with the dynamic scene of the New Jerusalem that John describes.

Gloriously, the Tree of Life appears in the vision of "the New" (22:1f). It is beside the river (Ezek 47:1) that flows from the Throne of God and the

---

5 Divination or *Theosis* is 'growth into God', to be "partakers of the divine nature" (2 Peter 1:4). It is the major goal of human life, made possible by Christ.
6 For a further description here see V. Lossky, *The Mystical Theology of the Eastern Church*, p.227f.

Chapter Ten - Delighting in the Consummation

Lamb. The Tree is "on either side of the river", being generic for many trees; the leaves will be for the healing of the nations (v.7). At last the full effect of Christ's sacrifice that inaugurated God's peace in the world and that broke the cycle of war and violence is brought forth into being. The luscious, environmental depiction represents the flowering of the work of Christ, which had been manifested so far in the witness of the saints and martyrs, of the many and varied servants of the Lamb. The depiction is so serene and wide; peace-makers find their joy and their rest and war-mongers are put to flight.

In addition, the picture here, powerfully yet gently, evokes hope for the pain and decay of the environment, providing an energising of those who work diligently for its sustainability and renewal.

The vision is seen by John as he lived on Patmos. We enter the vision especially by means of participating in the Sunday eucharistic celebration that gives "a taste of the things to come" (Hebr 6:4). We are challenged to hold and live the vision in enduring courageous discipleship, witnessing ourselves to these truths, in solidarity with refugees and other groups who are oppressed as their courage "rubs off" on us.

At this point in this final chapter I wish to pose two questions. One question is to ask, is the focus of Revelation being directed towards the universe as a whole or is it directed towards planet earth only?

The other question is to ask, can we move tentatively beyond the symbolism of John towards a rational perspective that could accompany the symbolic portrayal?

Firstly, John's vision is universal in its imagery, stars fall from the heavens, etc.. Written during a pre-Copernican period of history the book sees the earth at the centre of the universe. It sees the universe being involved in deconstruction and reconstruction, centred on the earth. But can the whole scene, as we today read it, be interpreted to refer exclusively to planet earth and human life upon it? The question here is difficult and to a degree is "academic". It is true to say, however, that John's main concern is for this world, its judgment and salvation. We have seen that the cosmic imagery of cataclysms is symbolic. Hence, we can say that the universal imagery is in reference to planet earth and its future. What God is doing elsewhere in the cosmos is God's business.

Secondly, we may well be asking a question about what can be said, after receiving the imagery, in terms of rational, systemic statements. We have been exposed to an array symbolism and allegory[7]. We have seen in ch.1 that the purpose of apocalyptic genre is to describe things that are beyond rational understanding. However, is it possible for us to delve beneath the images and posit an understanding in more rational terms, or we may say, as a logical corollary, of what is claimed as truth?

A certain hesitancy pops up at this point. We wish to maintain that apocalyptic thought as symbolic writing is the better vehicle of conveying what is deemed to be true when dealing with future realities and how they impinge on the present. John has been given the vision; he is a prophet of God, thereby implying that symbolism is the appropriate way to present the mysteries of the present and future. Story and symbol focus the reader into a more relational, humble condition before the providence of Almighty God, compared to a rational approach which facilitates and maybe tempts the reader to control that which is read and resist maintaining a receptive, modest mind in relation to it.

At the same time the challenge to find a way to offer a more rational sense of the topic could be helpful, to subsist beneath the authority of the vision in its written form - and to do so within the framework of doctrine and the scope of the Christian scriptures.

Such an attempt can be undertaken by observing the thought of John Zizioulas, a theologian in the Greek Orthodox Church.[8] He writes of Being as Love. God is (ultimate) Being and the being of God is Love. "Love

---

[7] Allegory can be understood as a sub-set of symbolism in that an allegory is a figure of speech that functions as suggestive of something else (e.g. Lamb, Beast, Book of Life...); symbolism is more general and polyvalent whereby words, images, etc. are 'thrown together' (lit. meaning in Gk) in pointing to another reality.

[8] See his book, *Being as Communion*. Zizioulas in his writing here is not directly attempting to make a connection with Revelation. He is writing on the basis of exploring basic doctrine. I am utilizing his approach.

Chapter Ten - Delighting in the Consummation

as God's mode of existence constitutes God's Being." Human beings are created on the basis of the Love of God, to live within that love. Stepping outside the divine domain precipitates death, the inroad of evil and the legacy of sin expressed in jealousy, greed and violence. The being of God as Love yearns to heal human wounded-ness, yet humanity's warring spirit is opposed to God, as the four horsemen of the Apocalypse convey (Rev6). Positing Love (although the word itself is scarcely used in the text of John) as the controlling category in Revelation[9] brings the book in line with the gospels and the compassionate ministry of Jesus.

The key question then presents itself in relation to fallen humanity and the structures of society that evolve: How can God break the tyranny of sin and violence (the Domination System)? God breaks it in the incarnation of his Son, his life, death and resurrection. The scene then is set for the final drama with the persistence of Love in the world to redeem humanity and the created order. Love is patient... it bears all things, hopes all things; love never ends (I Corinth. 13:4,7,8).

Revelation can fit within this systematic framework. As well as being based on a standpoint of Love Revelation is a book, a letter, of judgment. It has been so misunderstood in this regard throughout much of western Christian history. Judgment is to do with sifting, dividing the true from the untrue, the just from the unjust, the wheat from the tares. But God's judgment whilst it is unwavering, is also loving and patient, bears all things – focused on the crucifixion of Christ. At the same time, God's loving does not mean it is soft and compromising of God's Self.

Throughout all of humanity's self-interested endeavours the divine will persists in order to restore. Judgment has occurred in Jesus Christ's teaching, and in his death. The many who will respond to the Spirit's call to come to the harmony and the fullness of Love in the New Jerusalem is the result of Love's endeavor, Love's expense. There will be the restoration of "the many" and the natural environment will be renewed

---

9 "Love" is not a major word mentioned in Rev. It appears in verses: 1:5 ("unto Him who loves us"), 3:9, 12:11.

to be made whole. In the mercy of God, Love can still have its severe side, an accountable side (see a further discussion in ch.11).

We can therefore sense that this more systematic thinking is in line with John's presentation.

In the chapters of this book so far we have delved into the vision of Revelation and explored many of its meanings. The legitimate place of the book in the canon of scripture, although it has been questioned through the course of history, remains secure as the authoritative vision of God's final purpose in the present and the future, based on the resurrection of Christ: "isn't it wonderful that the Lamb defeated the Beast."

Broader Considerations

Chapter Eleven

Love and Justice

The vision of John is pitched against the gross injustices of Rome and her empire in which, strangely to us, there were philosophers who frequented the imperial court.

Cicero was one of them. He lived and wrote in the first century B.C. He disliked Caesar's dictatorship and the shift in power away from the elected senate. Rome had been sensitive about issues of supreme power as indicated in the senate's forbidding of the title "king". But "emperor" became a title that was permitted. Cicero wrote the *Res Republica,* a stoic attempt to provide a clear ethical perspective on public power. Later he delivered an oration against Mark Antony, after which he was captured and put to death.

In the next century the court philosopher, Seneca, suffered a similar fate after his upholding of public ethics when Nero sent him a message to commit suicide, which he promptly did. The tradition of justice as honoured thought was now in danger.

Justice in Roman thought, based as it was on Greek philosophy, was deemed the queen of virtue ethics. Someone who was conspicuous in virtue without being just was not only a flawed individual but was dangerous as well.[1] Cicero saw Caesar as belonging to this category.

Love has its place in classical thinking but it was not considered a virtue. Storge (family love), eros, philia (friendship) and agape constituted the notion of love. Eros and philia were spurs to virtue. Christianity changed this philosophical thinking with love being considered as the reflection of God's love, and consequently was regarded as a virtue. St Paul gave the definition of agape love: it suffers long, does not envy, does not flaunt itself ... seeks not its own (1 Corinth 13:4-7).

---

1 See Andreas Kinneging, *The Geography of Good and Evil*, p.156f.

In his teaching Jesus orientated love most poignantly towards the love of enemies. But – we note especially with Revelation in mind – loving one's enemies does not mean that we are to love evil. Christianity's discovery of agape (self-giving) love did not mean that the new religion and its emerging philosophical thinking broke with the classical notion of virtue ethics, but in a sense it built on it. Love and justice are seen as having central significance but love is supreme.

We may ask, does love according to the Christian understanding make justice redundant? Love God and do what you like, wrote St Augustine. There is some high ideal here of a deeply committed focus on the love of God which then flows into all of life. But in the course of normal life just laws and boundaries are in fact required. As a compassionate court judge knows, there have to be limits established for the management of human communities so that people can live together as peacefully as possible. The judge must deal justice in relation to the wrong action of a perpetrator for the good of society – at the same time as feeling pity for that person who is sentenced. So love is not a sufficient perspective for human life; justice is also needed.

These reflections bring us to the realisation that the two qualities cannot replace each other. We find too that this is true of the divine disclosure in the scriptures. There is God's justice and there is God's love. The modern pathway of unpacking the nature of God's love often emphasises the unconditional love that we see in the gospels. Jesus is seen there welcoming sinners and the most unloved in the society of that time. He heals the deeply wounded spirit and teaches about the nature of healing forgiveness.

When we turn to the Johannine literature we find explicit emphases about the nature of love in statements like "God so loved the world that he gave his only Son" (John 3:16), and "God is love and those who live in love live in God" (1 John 4:17). However Revelation, being considered traditionally a part of the Johannine literature, does not include an explicit focus on God's love. In the gospels the passion of Christ makes the point clear: God loves humanity and the creation to the extremes of

Chapter Eleven - Love and Justice

love as we see the arms of Jesus outstretched on the cross: Father, forgive them for they don't know what they are doing.

How then is the unconditional love of God represented in Revelation, if at all? It is explicit in the other Johannine literature but in John's vision we can say that it is present but not quite explicit. It overshadows and overarches the apocalyptic narrative in what can be described as an interweaving of love and justice. Love is imaged foremost in the figure of the Lamb, as gentle and forgiving. His "wrath" (6:16) is to be identified as his determination to see God's loving purposes triumph.

Love *and* justice actually appear in the figure of the Lamb, thus giving a clearer picture of his "wrath" in terms of desire to see a just outcome for the world. The trumpets and the bowls alert us to God's justice, providing warnings to our "thick sculls" to see and know what is at hand in the decision of God to bless the ministry of the Lamb and his followers, and to guide the world on its path through deconstruction to reconstruction. The alerts of justice are accompanied by the continual impulses of divine love, as the bystanders are saved from the burning city (ch.18) and all are brought to the final just and merciful judgment at the end of time.

John's whole vision is undergirded by the hidden authority of the sovereign God characterised by God's loving justice. Symbolically, God's love is ablaze and burns with a fire on earth to guide, purify and redeem, a scenario which also can be described as God's justice. The sovereign God works with a totally loving purpose and with a cosmic stance of justice. Like the compassionate judge God sees that justice must reign in his creation so that all creatures and living things in the New Creation are at the caring service of each other. And this is pictured in the New Jerusalem.

We see then this Christian form of apocalyptic trajectory in Revelation holding love and justice together in a creative tension. How does this play out in the Christian life of following the Lamb – as we recognise the healing power of unconditional love which lies at the heart of Christian experience and which urges us to work for justice, to stand against all that is unloving and to love the unlovely, as we have been loved?

Revelation informs us of the harsh realities of the world in which we find ourselves. At this point it is good to turn back to the gospels to provide us with a creative blend of how to forgive our enemies and at the same time stand against evil and injustice. I give two examples which are in tune with the character of Revelation. (I lean on Walter Winks' work here.)

To turn the other cheek in Matthew's gospel is not simply a command to be submissive, a doormat of being a coward and complicit in the face of wrong. Let the context at the time explain. *Do not set yourself up against someone who wrongs you. If someone slaps you on the right cheek turn and offer them the left* (5:39). I could hit you on the right cheek if I used a left hook, but that would be impossible in Semitic society because the left hand was used only for unclean tasks. The only way I could hit you on the right cheek would be with the back of the hand. Now the back of the hand is not a blow intended to injure. It is a symbolic blow usually from a master to a slave. It is intended to remind you of your place in society. By turning the other cheek, you are defiantly saying to the master, I refuse to be humiliated by you any longer. I am a human being just like you. I am a child of God.

In a similar manner the advice to walk two miles with the man in authority (Roman soldier) who makes you walk one mile (Matt. 5:41-42) is best understood from the context. The soldiers often had to move quickly and carry heavy packs. The military law made it permissible for a soldier to force a civilian to carry the pack, but only one mile and there were mile markers on every Roman road. If a civilian was forced to carry the pack more than one mile, the soldier was in contravention of the military code that was strictly enforced. Jesus is saying, keep going past the mile marker! If this situation is seen the soldier then is in trouble. Jesus is teaching his listeners how to take the initiative away peaceably from their oppressors and within the situation of that old order, find a new way of being.

Chapter Eleven - Love and Justice

Both of these examples suggested ways of behaving that expose injustice but in a peaceful, love-based manner, in a form of resistance. We can imagine that this is the kind of creatively courageous behaviour that the leaders of the seven churches of Asia recommended after receiving John's letter. Similarly, Jesus' teaching here provides inspiration for acting justly and in a love-based, nonviolent way in today's world.

CHAPTER TWELVE

The Apocalyptic Heart

The apocalyptic heart is....

- that heart which believes and delights in God's plan to bring all things to their completion and glorious consummation, the unfolding of Beauty in a mutuality of holy love, in which the massive evils present in the world are overcome.
- that heart which yearns with alertness to see just and peaceful relationships – spiritual, personal, communal, national and global.
- that heart which is aware that there is no end to the cycle of human misery save by means of the break-in to history of the Christ, the Lamb, who is the Power of Love.
- that heart which beats with those who see no human solution to the pain of people in their community or nation and the pain of the environment and daily prays, "Lord, your Kingdom come."
- that heart which knows there can be life-giving initiatives of Grace in the present, often in near impossible circumstances, that are signs of the Kingdom to come.
- that heart which is focused, penitent, generous, expectant and prayerful for a better world.
- that heart which believes in the quickening action of the Holy Spirit (the down-payment of the Kingdom) to guide, break down and construct.
- that heart which speaks readily to others of the "hope that is within" (1 Pet 3:15).
- that heart that is immersed in the Church's eucharistic life and participates in it as a foretaste of the things to come.
- that heart that believes at the End, when evil is finally defeated,

there will be the Last Judgment in which Almighty God's justice will be shown foremost in mercy.

Therefore, those who seek to live this way –

- associate closely with the spiritually like-minded: Do not be afraid, little flock, for the Kingdom of God is among you - Luke 17:21.
- view death as the entry into Paradise to be resting in Jesus until the Great Day.
- embrace with imagination the symbolic domain of New Testament apocalyptic and faithfully interpret it in order to hold fast the conviction of God's future.
- honour the martyrs and the saints as examples and intercessors at the Gate of Heaven, maintaining belief in the Communion of Saints as precious for life's continuing journey.
- realise that "apocalyptic" movies, computer games, artistic expression and literature of future cataclysms are often without the hope that deeply apocalyptic hearts possess.
- call for urgent spiritual change in the face of the contemporary "apocalyptic" environmental and other threats to our planet and its peoples.
- turn to avenues of contemplation in the knowledge that the Vision of God and God's Kingdom can be accessed through depths of prayer in the present as it will be fully revealed in the future.

Chapter Thirteen

Inquiry: Nick's Questions

To assist in the evolving of this book I travelled to Patmos in October 2014. My son, Nick, then 30, accompanied me. Each of us had interests of a literary nature to pursue. Mine of course was the text of Revelation; his was Homer's *The Odyssey* which is also set in the Aegean where the hero Odysseus makes his journey homeward after his exploits at Troy.

We read each other's texts before the trip. Nick doesn't consider himself a committed believer but his interest in John's vision has been quite strong for some years. I enjoyed reading Homer's tale and so the scene was set for a few interesting exchanges during our trip.

Patmos attracts many tourists so we decided to stay for twelve days on an adjacent island called Lipsi and commute by ferry to Patmos for some day trips. On arrival at our island cottage Nick gave me a photocopied extract to read. He had already read the document. It was a comparison of Odysseus and Jesus as great heroes. I found it fascinating, especially the apocalyptic comparison between the two heroes in which the author noted an apocalyptic outcome of crisis and judgment in relation to each of the heroes. Odysseus' apocalyptic outcome was to return to his home island of Ithaca where he had been king and kill the suitors who had taken control as well as sought to woo his wife, Penelope, and spend the island's resources on luxurious festivities. The apocalypse of Jesus however is different: in terms of what he taught, it is projected to a future time.

There is considerable violence in both the stories of *The Odyssey* and the gospels. The difference in the way violence is presented in each and "who does what to whom" became a major thought in my reflection on the comparison. *The Odyssey* continued to engage Nick during our trip. He took the book with him to read as he relaxed on some of the beaches of the island. It is a tale of powerful imagery and exciting adventures, including Odysseus having possibly stayed for seven years on Lipsi itself.

Nick travelled with me to Patmos on the second of my three day visits. After this trip he started to re-read Revelation. The fact that he had given me the extract of comparing Jesus and Odysseus indicated to some extent at least where he was coming from in his own thinking. He then posed some questions to me after his second reading. His questions were of great interest to me as they were spontaneously rendered during morning reading periods.

Here are some of the questions and my attempted answers.

Why do they fall down and worship? The question arose from reading the opening heavenly scene in Rev4. I was surprised by the question, thinking to myself, it is obvious why people worship God, whether they are in heaven or on earth. Then I realised that inquirer-type questions can appear as "left-field" or odd to long-term believers who tend to take basic questions for granted. Yet they are critically important questions and require helpful responses to the person inquiring. My reply was something like, God should be worshipped because God creates and redeems.

Immediately I felt unhappy with my reply. I knew it was not meeting Nick at a point of his thinking. Later I thought that a simple, initial answer would be to say that the reason for the people's heavenly worship is that they have been liberated, they know Christ's liberation like Moses after passing through the Red Sea. They express joyful praise – they are in a state of awe. This is what is meant in Revelation at this point with the worship of the twenty-four elders.

As Nick was reading the whole text it might have been good to say too that Revelation revolves around worship. Its opposite in the text is idolatry, powerfully represented in bowing down to and obeying the imperial powers.

That would have been a better, albeit layered answer. But I think it would have been a more satisfying answer than what I gave.

A second question was a very understandable one for either believers or non-believers to ask: Why "the wrath of the Lamb" (Rev6:16)? It's

Chapter Thirteen - Inquiry: Nick's Questions

such a strange and severe image. I didn't do too badly responding to this question, at least in my own estimation of the situation! "Wrath" here means Christ's anger-type determination to see justice and goodness triumph; he stands strongly yet gently – not in a state of human anger – against the evil powers that destroy.

I thought after these two answers, gosh, it's hard to respond to one's own grown up children on matters of faith. I have three in their thirties, Nick being the youngest. At the same time I appreciated him freely asking questions to do with faith. Then there was a third question which has involved me in a few discussions since with some friends and colleagues.

Finishing his second reading of the text, Nick asked, "Will I be let in to the New Jerusalem?" There is always a level of deep sincerity to such questions, even if they are put somewhat casually. I was nearly floored. Well, I replied, I guess the clue is in the text itself. It depends on what is written about us in the books and what we have done in our lives. I felt that whilst it was more or less accurate, this was a cold, clinical response. Sometime afterwards I thought that a better reply would be to say, the New Jerusalem is such a magnificent, inspirational vision and we are offered grace to go there.

This third question loitered in my mind and on return to Australia I fielded it with a few folk whom I knew and respected and did so on separate occasions. "Did you tell him that he is already there?" one said to me. I felt that this was unsatisfactory. It was a "grace" statement like God loves you before you even know it. I valued the perspective although it wasn't enough. A priest friend then suggested as a reply to the question with, Do you want to go there? That's good, I thought. It's a really genuine, engaging reply that opens up further questions or considerations. A third person offered another counter question, Do you want to strive to make it [to the New Jerusalem]? This I also liked, for it invites taking up responsibility to go on the journey – a journey to be graced by the vision of the New Jerusalem.

I reflected on why it is difficult to give good answers on the spot. In the past I have been involved in group inquiry,[1] a mix of non-believers and believers, meeting together to help each other find the way by sharing helpful responses. People often find the step-by-step answers they need in this setting. At the same time it is good and necessary often to respond to questions of faith wherever and whenever they are asked.

The other reflection I had is that reading Revelation usually has not been regarded as an inquirer's text. One of the gospels has been seen in the past as the best choice. The Apocalypse of John is complex and therefore it has been understandably left to consider at a later stage. However in today's world of exposure to moving images and an interest among young people in visionary, poetic thinking, Revelation may well have more of a place for the purposes of asking basic questions about the Christian faith.

Revelation as a document is complex. No-one disagrees with that as a basic description of what John's letter is like. A few days before leaving our island Nick and I gave a rendering of our own texts in our own words and without notes. Each presented to an audience of one! Nick gave his clearly and with enthusiasm. I wandered through mine since to present Revelation as a story is not really possible - an apocalyptic narrative, yes, but not a normal story. I bought and lit seven candles to assist in the telling and moved them around according to what part of the narrative I was presenting – churches, seals, bowls… I received an honest reply at the end of the presentation – it's disjointed and confusing, it needs a frame. This response triggered some necessary thinking on my part – a framing of the text which I wrote the next day and has been included in the introduction of this book.

---

1 See *Taking the Plunge* (by the author) Wipf & Stock 2010

CHAPTER FOURTEEN

Life-Themes

Four guiding principles are pivotal for the paragraphs that follow. They help in gearing the nature of apocalyptic thinking towards the task of living.

1. **The gift of the Holy Spirit** in the between-time of Christ's first and second Coming orientates us to the fullness of the Kingdom, bestowing in advance, as down-payments, conversion, challenge, courage, risk-taking, deep comfort and wisdom.
2. **The images** of John's apocalyptic vision provide a territory of inspiration beyond rational thinking: (major images) angels, the Lamb, the Beast, light and darkness…; (specific images) the four horsemen, saints under the altar, the Dragon thrown in the lake of fire…
3. **Urgency** that the apocalyptic vision involves and which embraces us as we enter the vison: the urgency of belief, prayer and action.
4. **The overlapping aeons.** An aeon constitutes one of the longest conceivable divisions in time. We now live in the overlap of the old and new: the two aeons whereby the Kingdom has been inaugurated in the event of Christ and yet the old order and its ways persist (1 Corin 2:6, 2 Corin 4:4).

Apocalyptic and …
… Youth

"You should be a communist when you are young to activate your passion to change the world." So it has been said. It is much better and more lasting to gain the spiritual resources of God's grace to change the world and turn to the resurrection of Jesus and the vision of the New Heaven and the New Earth. You will discover the energy of the Holy Spirit and also will want to speak of "the hope that is within you" to others.

... Mid-Life

Immersed in work, raising a family and paying the home mortgage… and maybe coping with the crisis of who I really am and what I am doing… I can easily become absorbed within matters that belong to the old aeon. But I can lift my head and see a wider horizon that is the wonder of the in-coming Kingdom, the new aeon. Signs of it may be seen even in my marriage and family. This is not just a call to think positively but to perceive more deeply and widely.

... Ageing

Slowing down can be a blessing. We can take time to see and savour the signs of the Kingdom that we have been a part of over the years, whether by our own contribution or by others … to develop a spirit of lasting thankfulness amidst doctor appointments and the silent stretches in our present lives … to ease into simple, gentle forms of service in the family and beyond, and to take time to engage in contemplative prayer.

... Approaching Death

"I wonder what it will be like," an old man said to me once about passing through death. Such a simple and free-from -fear statement, I thought. We know we shall have to give an account. But mercy is the last word, which must include our mercy towards others. The letter of James provides a summary note on how we should prepare: *speak and act as those who are to be judged by the law of liberty; for judgment without mercy will be shown to those who have not been merciful; mercy triumphs over judgment* (2:13). God gives us our precious pre-death time not just to get our finances in order but more especially to work on the motions of our hearts. In this inner work God's grace abounds.

... Funerals

Angels, martyrs and saints hold a strong presence in John's vision. They are a helpful focus at the time of farewell. Eulogies and sharing memories need to be carefully balanced with the primary focus of commending the person to God. Let us recognise the rich mystery at hand – the company of angels and saints to assist the departed person on the pathway to the New Jerusalem. The mourners present as prayers must play their part in the assisting. Acknowledge the body of the deceased as that which intricately is bound up with who the person was and is. The *In Paradisum* sung in relation to the bodily person provides a wholesome rite:

> May the angels lead you into Paradise;
> may the martyrs come to welcome you and take you to the holy city, the new and eternal Jerusalem.
> May choirs of angels welcome you and lead you to the bosom of Abraham;
> and where Lazarus is poor no longer may you find eternal rest.

... Spiritual Growth

The spiritual life doesn't just happen. It requires discipline. Then after a while we experience what the desert fathers and mothers of the fourth and fifth centuries called *acedia*: dryness or boredom, the struggle to go on. But it is along this path of patience and trust that small or large, inner apocalypses occur; these are the moments when the Holy Spirit eases our burden, comforts us, and maybe presents a challenge or floods our souls with love.

... Dreaming

Our night dreams can be put into the basket of the Christian apocalyptic dream. Individual dreams are either encouraging or challenging, or both. With the help of wise counsel the Holy Spirit can guide us on the inner level of our being. Understood dreams enrich our sense of purpose as we make our journey within the great Dream of the coming Kingdom.

... Disaster

After the tragedy of a tsunami religious commentators in the press vary in their opinions. Most muslims say it is God's will; fundamentalist Christians remark that it is the judgment of God upon human sin. However, there is a more authentically Christian response which is in terms of the event being a reminder to us that "the whole creation waits in eager expectation ... to be freed from its bondage" (Rom 8:20-21).

Every disaster is a sign of the last days. They remind us again that God's judgment has come to the world yet the disaster is nothing to do with whether the victims individually sinned or not. A new made-whole creation is promised by God. Such an event calls us to active prayer and service because the "times, they are a'changin'".

... Failure (?)

A friend of mine is about to retire from lifelong medical service in a developing country. His heart is heavy with the lack of progress in health in that country and with the extent of corruption in government circles. The weight of these issues is concentrated in his mind as he looks back over the decades. He needs the company of friends to draw out the signs of the Kingdom that he has been a part of – lovely, often not highly visible signs in which individuals were cured, small steps forward occurred, some younger medics caught a positive vision... In our fight against the principalities and powers (Ephes. 6) we see failures. More importantly though, as people of faith, let us focus on the living signs of the Kingdom in whatever our long-term work and commitments have been. They may not be grand but we can recognise their significance.

... Gentleness

The middle-aged monk that I conversed with at the monastery on the island of Patmos (see ch. 7) was a kind of icon of gentleness. Sitting together on the low stone wall outside the monastery chapel he spoke softly but with a warm firmness about the apocalyptic way, as he understood it within monastic living. The apocalypse is a map providing a pathway between good and evil, based on love. I wondered, had he given this little talk to many other pilgrims before talking to me? If he had, there was no indication of it, for his eyes and voice were full of freshness. A calm and caring gentleness.

... and Trauma

Trauma arises from various backgrounds. The liturgy of the Sunday eucharist is a wonderful, holy vehicle of bearing up wounded bodies and souls. As we are present at the breaking of the bread and pouring of the wine we then receive the broken body and poured-out blood of Christ:

Chapter Fourteen - Life-Themes

broken bread for broken people... to heal gradually and purposefully... to eat and drink until he comes again. The One like a Son of Man (Rev1) still stands among the churches even today.

... Relationships

Let the light in on relationships: allow for openings in your thinking about others to whom you have been bonded and with whom you may be experiencing some difficulties. See them more broadly and deeply than what immediately comes to heart and mind. The inner light that then shines is that which enlightens the way of the saints, the servants of the Lamb, breeding appreciation, forbearance and a more generous love.

... Saturday Evenings

Light a white candle on Saturday evenings and place it centrally in your home. It will shine in preparation for the weekly celebration of Christ's resurrection the next day and of the sure and certain hope of the Consummation to come.

... Music

Recently I listened to Arvo Paert's *Cantus in memoriam Benjamin Britten*. Paert's music often attracts people who don't normally listen to classical music. This particular work is a sustained, broadening crescendo into an imagined vast and succulent landscape, a six and a half minute orchestration marked by the sounding of a bell, a composition of hopefulness, moving towards an all-inclusive end-point. Do you recognise a work of music that provides you with a well-imagined sense of the Christian promised future and supports your apocalyptic heart?

Glossary

Armeggedon	Scene of final conflict between the nations.
Cataclysm	A deluge, a political or ecological upheaval
Consummation	The culmination of history, the fulfillment of God's purposes
Eschatology	Study of the Last Things or End-times.
Gentile	Non-Jewish person or people
Immolation	Victim put to death as a sacrifice.
Liturgy	(literally) "Work of the people"; the Church's order of worship, especially the eucharist.
Millenarian	Belief in the thousand years reign of Christ on earth preceding his Second Coming; expectancy of these events to take place (chronologically) soon.
Mystical	Spiritual apprehension of truth beyond rational understanding.
Polyvalent	More than one interpretation of a text whereby the interpretations are held side by side.

Selected Bibliography

Bauckham, Richard. *The Theology of the Book of Revelation* Cambridge: Cambridge, 1993

Berkoff, Hendrikus. *The Christian Faith* Michigan: Eerdmans, 1985

Boesak, Allan A. *Comfort and Protest, The Apocalypse from a South African Perspective* Philadelphia: Westminster, 1987

Boring, Eugene M. *Revelation* Louisville: John Knox Press, 1989

Boxall, Ian. *Revelation: Vision and Insight* London: SPCK, 2002

Daly, Robert J. (Ed.) *Apocalyptic Thought in Early Christianity* Michigan: Holy Cross Orthodox Press, 2009

Ellul, Jacques. *Apocalypse, The Book of Revelation* New York: Seabury, 1979

Hopko, Thomas. *Apocalypse, The Book of Revelation within the Orthodox Christian Tradition* CD Lectures, St Vladimir's Press, New York

Lee, Dorothy. *Hallowed by Truth and Love, Spirituality in the Johannine Literature* Melbourne: Mosaic Press, 2011

Lossky, Vladimir. *The Mystical Theology of the Eastern Church* Cambridge: James Clark, 1968

Richard, Pablo. *Apocalypse, A People's Commentary on the Book of Revelation* Eugene: Wipf & Stock, 2008

Wainwright, Geoffrey. *Eucharist and Eschatology* Ohio: Epworth, 2002

Wink, Walter. *Engaging the Powers* Mineapolis: Fortress, 1992

Wright, N. T. *Surprised by Hope* New York: HarperCollins, 2008